Glorious 1911

and Bradford City's Golden Age, 1908-15

David Pendleton

David Pendleton was born a goal kick away from Bradford (Park Avenue) at St Luke's Hospital. Despite that inauspicious start he became a lifelong supporter of Bradford City. He was editor of The City Gent fanzine between 1997-2001 and in 2003 he co-organised Bradford City's centenary exhibition at Bradford Industrial Museum. He helped establish the bantamspast museum at Valley Parade in 2005 and is the curator of the museum. David has an MA in social history from Leeds Metropolitan University and is currently a PhD student researching the development of professional sport in Bradford 1863-1915.

Typeset by Highlight Type Bureau Ltd, Bradford BD8 7HB

Cover design by Simon Frater and printed by
Hart and Clough Ltd, Cleckheaton, West Yorkshire BD19 4TQ

A bantamspast publication
PO Box 307, Shipley, BD18 9BT
www.bantamspast.co.uk

ISBN No 978 0 9566984 0 7

First printed 2010

Contents

Acknowledgements

Many people have contributed to the research and production of this book. Without them this centenary celebration would never have come to fruition. As well as the individuals listed below I would like to thank the staff of Bradford Central Library for their help and patience. Without the local studies department this book would have simply never seen the light of day. We should support and value our library services.

Chris Ambler (additional research), John Ashton (artwork and project management), Mick Callaghan (additional research and support), John Dewhirst (proof reading and project management), Andrew George (loan of memorabilia), David Markham (additional research and support), Mark Neale (project support), Andrew Pickles (additional research).

David Pendleton

Internet Resources

www.bantamspast.co.uk
The website of the bantamspast museum providing an online historical resource.

www.jimmy-speirs.co.uk
Website dedicated to City's FA Cup hero.

www.paraders.co.uk
Retro Bradford City enamel badges and cuff links. Authentic reproductions of historic crests and designs including releases to commemorate the FA Cup centenary. Certain items are being sold on ebay (seller identity: Paraders) including commemorative Glorious 1911 scarves. All available to purchase in bantamspast before kick-off on match days.

Events Commemorating Glorious 1911

Book launch and Bradford City historic film night, Pictureville Bradford on 21 November, 2010.

Glorious 1911 Exhibition, Bradford Industrial Museum from 9 April, 2011 to 12 June, 2011.

Commemorative dinner and historical evening, Midland Hotel Bradford on 26 April, 2011.

Visit to Bradford City WW1 players' war graves, France 2 to 6 June, 2011.

Bookings and further details from glorious1911@paraders.co.uk

Future bantamspast publications

We are planning to publish two further titles on the history of Bradford City and Valley Parade. Our next book will be released in October 2011 to mark the 125th anniversary of the first use of Valley Parade as a sports arena. To join our mailing list and be informed of future books contact glorious1911@paraders.co.uk or write to bantamspast, PO Box 307, Shipley BD18 9BT. News updates will be provided on www.bantamspast.co.uk

Foreword

John Dewhirst

The early history of Bradford City is quite remarkable not only for the fact that the football club was elected to the Football League in 1903 without ever having played a game but for the momentum of success that was achieved in so short a period of time. Promotion to Division One as champions of the second division in 1908 and then, after only eight seasons, finishing fifth in Division One and winning the FA Cup in 1910/11.

It was a momentum that would not be sustained, let alone repeated. The closest was the seven seasons of successive improvement between 1981-88 or indeed the two five year spells of successive improvement between 1927-32 and, more recently, 1995-2000. City supporters became more accustomed to years of decline and periods of mediocrity. The suffering of the last decade would have been recognisable to those who experienced the club's slide from Division One in 1922 to the anonymity of Division Three (North) in 1927 and back again to the lower divisions from 1937 to 1985.

If the FA Cup triumph did not guarantee future success for the club it did bring a degree of respectability. To those supporters who could remember 'Glorious 1911' it provided a ray of hope and a memory that fate had not always been so cruel. It says much that the back cover of the supporters' handbook published in October, 1927 to raise monies for the parent club had the same inscription ('Glorious 1911') on its rear cover as something of a rallying call. Above all, Bradford City's FA Cup triumph differentiated the club not only from most of its league rivals but more importantly, from Bradford (Park Avenue) FC. Undoubtedly the fact that City had won the FA Cup would have been regularly reminded to Avenue supporters.

It is difficult to comprehend the sense of pride that the FA Cup victory bestowed upon Bradford City and its supporters. In the mid seventies I met Sam Firth, a founder member of the City Supporters' Association in December, 1948 and subsequent president who later perished in the Valley Parade fire at the age of 86 years. I was struck by his passion for City although it was understandable given that the club had been such a big part of his life (he had also been on the books as an amateur player in the 1920's). It was the fund raising efforts of the likes of Sam Firth, Ken Gudgeon and Alan Hannah who kept the club alive in the immediate post-war era. For Sam Firth Bradford City AFC was

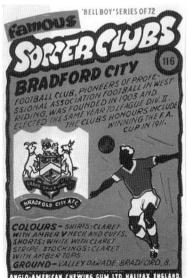

not a 'fourth division club' but former FA Cup holders and a sleeping giant that was down on its luck, whose rightful status was among those clubs against whom it had not played for decades. The reality was that even in 1910/11 Bradford City was never a club among equals as it challenged to establish itself within the elite ranks of English football. However, how poignant that Firth should die on the day when his cherished club ended a 48 year exile in the lower divisions.

The FA Cup victory thus served to reinforce the identity of City supporters. It was notable that even in 1974 when a merger with Bradford (PA) FC was being discussed and a new club name - Bradford Metro AFC – was suggested, that traditionalists argued against the proposal on the basis that it was Bradford City AFC who had won the FA Cup and whose name was engraved on its plinth. The same argument would have carried greater weight in the 1930's when Stanley Waddilove had proposed merger talks and a new super stadium at Odsal.

By the 1960s City supporters had little else to shout about. Apart from the FA Cup triumph in 1911 the club had managed promotion in only two seasons, 1907/08 and 1928/29. Little wonder then that the epithet 'FA Cup Winners 1911' featured on so many club souvenirs given that there was little else to mention. Outside of the city it was probably the only distinguishing feature to separate the two Bradford clubs and, crucially, when many began to question the merit of Bradford having two Football League clubs it could well have been a deciding factor. For example would Bradford (Park Avenue) have been successful in re-applying for re-election to the League in 1970 had it won the FA Cup sixty years' before? Hypothetical as it might be, I find it difficult to believe that Bradford City would have been voted out in similar circumstances.

Through to the 1950s FA Cup games continued to capture the imagination of the Bradford public. City fans dreamt of repeating the experience of 1911 whilst others would have hoped that the Park Avenue club might emulate its rivals at Valley Parade. Cup runs by either club were few and far between after 1920 and for the record, Avenue got as far as the quarter finals on three occasions, 1912/13, 1919/20 and 1945/46.

The 1975/76 season was memorable as it represented Bradford City's most successful FA Cup campaign since 1919/20 (when City had been beaten in the quarter-finals by Bristol City) and it was no mean feat for Bradford City (then a club languishing in the lower half of Division Four) to reach the sixth round stage and the last sixteen of the competition for the fifth time. It was an achievement that has not been repeated since and the prospect of Bradford City ever winning the FA Cup again is surely remote. Given the impact on the club's finances of its two seasons in the Premier League no-one would suggest emulating the experience of Portsmouth AFC to 'buy' FA Cup glory. Whilst 'Pompey' overcame more fancied rivals to win the FA Cup in 2008, at what price?

The FA Cup has lost much of its prestige and grandeur. It is difficult to generalise and suggest what the FA Cup winning triumph of 1910/11 means to contemporary supporters beyond a historical curio. It is quite possible that younger supporters will define Bradford City as a 'former Premier League club' in the same way that Sam Firth's generation would have defined City as former FA Cup winners. Again the reality was that in the Premier League we could not even pretend that Bradford City was a club among equals.

Last season the club introduced a solitary gold star above the crest on the team shirts to commemorate the fact that Bradford City had been FA Cup winners. In my opinion this only serves to invite ridicule and my preference would be to end the practice. I am not convinced that football shirt design is enhanced by gold stars and we might reflect that one hundred years later there have been a lot of other stars that we have not secured.

The momentum of the club's first decade was ultimately not sustained for financial reasons. Balance sheet constraints have been a recurring theme in the club's history and indeed they prompted the conversion from Manningham Rugby Club in 1903. The lack of funding meant that City's early successes were built on shallow foundations and for that reason the glory was fleeting.

It became apparent a long time ago that Bradford City would most likely never again reach those lofty heights achieved in 1910/11 but as Sam Firth would have pointed out, at least no-one could take away the fact that City had won the FA Cup and were the first holders of the current trophy. He might have added that many others, Bradford (PA) included, had tried and failed.

John Dewhirst is a life-long City supporter and collector of Bantams memorabilia (much of his collection is featured in this book). He was co-founder of The City Gent in 1984 and author of City Memories in 1997. He has collaborated on a number of historical projects with Dave Pendleton including Along the Midland Road (history of Valley Parade) in 1996 and various film events at Pictureville.

Introduction

Victorian Bradford was a rugby town. Indeed, the oval ball dominated the entire West Riding of Yorkshire. Thousands would flock to Park Avenue to see the all-conquering Bradford Rugby Club. Across town their smaller rival, Manningham Rugby Club, was emerging as a serious competitor. The predominantly working class club, with its distinctive claret and amber colours, actually overtook its cross-town rival for a handful of glorious years, winning Rugby Union's first league, the Yorkshire Senior Competition in 1894. Both Bradford clubs were founder members of the Northern Union – today's Rugby League – and Manningham were the new code's first champions in 1896.

The glory faded rapidly. Manningham were stubbornly loyal to the team that brought national fame to Valley Parade. The death of Valley Parade's first superstar, George Lorimer, aged only twenty-four, and the failure to replace the aging team, saw Manningham's crown slip away. Valley Parade was extended and improved at huge cost; the expectation of continued success and the staging of Yorkshire Cup finals at the ground proved to be folly. The debts from the ground redevelopment dragged the club into the new second tier of the Northern Union and without the income generated by the derby fixtures against Bradford the future looked bleak.

Local businessman Alfred Ayrton was invited onto the committee and when he became Manningham's president the club gained a renewed momentum. Ayrton quickly realised that without promotion to the top flight the club faced a struggle merely to survive. He cleared the debts

Manningham as a Rugby Union club photographed with
the Yorkshire Senior Competition Shield in 1894.

in January 1903 with an innovative competition that was a cross between archery and the national lottery. Numbered tickets were sold all over the country, and even as far afield as France. The numbers were placed on a huge revolving target and arrows fired to find the lucky winners. It was unconventional, but it worked. When local football enthusiasts looking to form a professional football club approached Ayrton, he could offer a ground, and club, clear of debt.

The switch to football wasn't without its critics, but Ayrton saw little alternative. Manningham faced a future of struggle as a second rate rugby club, or they could move into the national sport of football. In May 1903 Ayrton chaired a stormy meeting of Manningham's members when they voted decisively to become a football club. Ayrton even gave the new football club its name – Bradford City. The infant club was voted into the Football League without so much as having kicked a ball. There is little doubt that City's place in the second division had been

Alfred Ayrton

promised long before the election. It was a breakthrough for the Football League into an area previously dominated by rugby and Bradford City was West Yorkshire's first Football League club.

Bradford City still had to build a team from scratch. It was something of an achievement that they did so and during their first season they were never in any serious danger of having to apply for re-election. This was remarkable by any standards. When Ayrton retired from the presidency of Bradford City in 1907 the club was standing on the verge of promotion to the first division. His final act was to weigh up, and present to the club's members, a possible merger with the newly-formed Bradford (Park Avenue) FC. It was overwhelmingly rejected. The logic of ignoring Bradford's advances was seemingly confirmed when City won the second division championship in April 1908. Guided by their inspirational manager Peter O'Rourke, City began a decade that was to be their golden age but first they had to hold onto their hard-won top-flight status and, as ever, it was to be a dramatic fight.

CHAPTER ONE

A First Great Escape

1908/09

Given all that was to follow in Bradford City's golden age, it was perhaps fitting that they began their campaign against Newcastle United. City ran out at St James' Park for their first ever top-flight game sporting their new claret shirts with a broad amber yoke – a strip that was to become synonymous with the glories to come. It was an even game decided by a single goal ten minutes from time. During a Newcastle attack the ball seemed to go out of play and virtually all the players stopped, expecting the whistle. Jock Rutherford was free to put in an unchallenged cross and Colin Veitch shot low past Martin Spendiff in the City goal before anyone had chance to react. It was a frustrating way to begin life in Division One. Another single goal defeat at Middlesbrough the following Saturday had fans wondering what had happened to the Handley-McDonald-O'Rourke partnership that had terrorised defences in the second division.

Valley Parade's bow in Division One came on 12 September 1908, when Manchester City were

RAPID PHOTO. E.C.   McLEAN.   ROBERTS.   SPENDIFF.   FARREN.   WILSON.   5145
KELLING.   MENZIES.   MILLAR.   WISE.   HANDLEY.   HANGER.   WILLIAMS.   HARPER.
         ASST. TRAINER.   TRAINER.
CLARKE.   SMITH.   O'ROURKE.   CAMPBELL.   BARTLETT.   McDERMOTT.   ROBINSON.

LEAGUE COLOURS

BRADFORD CITY

B.D.V CIGARETTES

the visitors. Of course, Valley Parade had to be extended and improved to match the club's new status. Works to fully terrace the Nunn Kop and round off the Burlington Terrace corner had been completed, but construction of the new Midland Road stand had barely got underway. However, such was the crush on the Burlington Terrace side of the Nunn Kop that several hundred fans were allowed onto the Midland Road to ease the congestion. Former City favourite, and the club's first England international, Jimmy Conlin was given a tremendous ovation when he ran out with his Manchester City team mates. Conlin caused great anxiety with his tricky wing play, in particular his unorthodox tactic of suddenly cutting in and running along the edge of the eighteen yard line. City more than held their own, but midway through the first half an injury to George Handley disrupted City's plans. In those days before substitutions City were down to ten men and without the prolific forward many in the thirty thousand crowd were happy with the draw.

The architect of Valley Parade's transformation, Archibald Leitch, was at the game and immediately after the final whistle a meeting was held to attempt to learn lessons from the day. Several changes were made to the original plans. It was decided that the Midland Road stand would have no seating, the thinking being that 'two can stand where one can sit'. The seating in the Main Stand would be increased from twelve hundred to three thousand. The Paddock terracing would be taken right back to the South Parade wall and the wall built higher to prevent fans from climbing onto the stand roof.

Defeat at Liverpool the following Saturday, and yet another failure to find the net, dumped City onto the bottom of the table, a position they were to become all too familiar with. Still the enthusiasm among the fans was high. For the visit of Bury all the newly installed three thousand seats were taken and when Bob Campbell led City out from

Archibald Leitch

the tunnel, at the Burlington Terrace corner, over twenty-five thousand were packed into the ground. After only six minutes Willie Clarke exchanged passes with Wally Smith and shot City into

Valley Parade's inaugural Division One match v Manchester City, 12 September 1908.
Building work on the new Midland Road stand had barely begun.

the lead. Clarke and his fellow winger William Gould (newly signed from Glossop North End) ran riot as City cruised to a four goal victory. Despite the victory the club came in for criticism in the local press.

The pace of the development of the new Midland Road stand was the focus of the fans' ire. One letter writer thought that money was practically being thrown away. The first section of the stand had just reached pitch level and it was said 'if thirty men have put up that section in a certain number of weeks, we can safely assume that three times that number would have made the same progress with the stand from end to end.' Criticism was also made of the fact that the only exit from the 'Nunn Kop' was into the narrow Back Burlington Terrace. The club was obviously listening. For the Aston Villa match on 10 October a new large exit was made into Burlington Terrace itself. In order to ease congestion on the terraced section of the Main Stand, space was made available on the emerging Midland Road side for the 12s 6d members. Six steps along the entire length of the stand were ready, but there would be no cover. The move caused uproar with nightly letters to the local press. City president William Pollack replied appealing for members to 'show a little forbearance until the work can be completed'. The game against Villa saw thirty-five thousand jammed into Valley Parade. City fought for a creditable draw against one of the leading sides of the day.

The *Bradford Daily Argus* reporter 'Preceptor' made the first known reference to the 'Spion Kop' when commenting on City's match against Sunderland on 24 October. Until that date the great bank behind the goal had been known as Nunn Kop after its creator, City director John Nunn. Now, for the best part of 80 years, it would be the Spion Kop, so named after the South African hill where a large number of soldiers from the north of England had died during the Boer War.

It was recognised early in the season that if City were to survive in the top flight then new players would be required. In successive matches Peter Logan and George Chaplin made their debuts. Although both would make significant contributions to the club's future, the signing of

Evelyn Lintott

Logan was to prove to be one of the best investments in City's entire history.

The changes to Valley Parade continued on a weekly basis. When Blackburn Rovers visited on 7 November a balcony was in place on the club house on Burlington Terrace. It overlooked the pitch and would for years be used for presentations, as well as being a tremendous vantage point for club officials. Though part of the roof at last appeared on the Midland Road, it didn't stop the *Daily Argus* lamenting that the works were 'progressing in somewhat tortoise-like fashion'.

Despite the huge outlay on the ground, strengthening of the team continued apace. QPR and England international midfielder Evelyn Lintott caught the eye of City manager Peter O'Rourke. On 21st November 1908 O'Rourke travelled to London and met Lintott at Paddington station - Rangers were returning from a match at Swindon. He signed his man that night and Lintott joined City for over one thousand pounds. The transfer fee went a long way to helping QPR out of serious financial problems.

As a City player Lintott would go on to win four England caps, play in one North v South trial game and score for the Football League v Irish League. One of his England appearances was against Ireland at Park Avenue in 1909. Lintott was also a school teacher and during his first season at Valley Parade he continued to work at a school in Willesden in North London. The practicalities eventually prompted City to find him employment at 'Sports and Pastimes' - the makers of City's shirts. However, he expressed a wish to return to teaching and he secured a post at a school in Dudley Hill. Evelyn was also heavily involved with the emerging Players Union, known today as the PFA. From 1910-11 he was the head of the organisation. His brother Frederick Stacey Lintott - *Bradford Daily Telegraph* reporter 'Preceptor' - edited the Union's *Football Player Magazine*.

Despite the new blood City were still struggling at the foot of the division. To add to City's woes their lucky horseshoe mascot had been lost. The horseshoe had been hung in the players' train carriage when on their travels. It had been with them when they won the second division championship, so its loss was keenly felt. Up stepped the daughter of City director Tony Fattorini, whose company incidentally made the current FA Cup and Rugby League Challenge Cup. She gave the club a new mascot on 27 November 1908 - the eve of their home match against league leaders Everton. The mascot was a real live bantam. Its body was claret with an amber yoke, which matched the new shirt the club had adopted at the start of the season. The little bird even had white legs, the same colour as the player's shorts. As the *Bradford Daily Argus* commented: "Newcastle United have their magpie, Derby a ram, West Brom a throstle, Hull City a tiger and Leeds City a peacock. But now, Bradford City have a real live claret and amber bantam." From that moment on City were known as the Bantams.

The new mascot immediately brought with it a change in fortunes. A creditable 1-1 draw with Everton was followed in early December by what was entitled as 'the Great Awakening'. Leicester Fosse were thrashed 4-1 and such was the relief that a large crowd cheered the team when they arrived back at the Midland station (since renamed Forster Square). The following

Saturday Frank O'Rourke scored after only two minutes as Arsenal were demolished at Valley Parade. However, City were still firmly rooted to the bottom of the table. The fans were in great heart though and before the Christmas Day match against Bristol City there was a 'remarkable display of vocal power'. The Spion Kop and the rest of the ground tried to out-sing one another with seasonal hymns. Apparently, the Spion Kop won, but when the City players emerged from the tunnel the whole ground erupted into a chorus of 'Hello Hello'. Though they suffered yet another single goal defeat, victory – courtesy of a Frank O'Rourke strike in the return fixture at Bristol City – on Boxing Day lifted City off the foot of the table for the first time.

The first game of the 1909 saw the Bantams playing Manchester City at a fog-bound Hyde Road. With the scores tied at 3-3, and the light fading fast, the last five minutes were played in near darkness. When the home side won a corner City's keeper Martin Spendiff didn't see the ball until it appeared in the air in front of his goal. The ball fell to the feet of former City favourite Jimmy Conlin who scored from close range to win the match. It was the beginning of a run of four successive defeats that dumped City back onto the bottom of the table. The reverse at third bottom Bury caused the *Daily Argus* to lament 'all hope has vanished'.

James Comrie

As always in football, hope sprang eternal when City won at West Brom in the FA Cup and then caused a sensation by defeating the cup favourites Aston Villa. It was a stunning, if bad tempered, victory at Villa Park. James Comrie deliberately tripped Villa's Harry Hampton. Though nicknamed 'Happy Harry' the Villa forward leapt up and took a swinging kick at City's centre-half. Comrie calmly lifted his foot and took the blow on the sole of his boot. Comrie's coolness probably saved Hampton from being sent off. However, just as the City faithful were dreaming of a change in fortunes, successive single goal defeats at the hands of Sunderland in the FA Cup and league, saw the gloom gathering over Valley Parade once more. With teams directly above City finding form, there was a danger that they would be cast adrift at the bottom. Indeed, despite a creditable draw at Blackburn Rovers, City found themselves six points behind second bottom Nottingham Forest. Though City had a game in hand, in the days of two points for a victory, City's predicament was serious.

Despite the worsening situation the annual club trip to Sheffield Wednesday saw seven trains making the short journey to the steel city. Club trips were common prior to the Great War and City's were chosen by a ballot of supporters. Many fans saved up all season, and though large numbers regularly watched City away from home, for many fans the club trip was their only opportunity to follow their favourites away from Valley Parade. Sheffield Corporation laid on special trams to meet the six trains that arrived at Sheffield Midland station. The fans on the single train run by the Great Northern Railway Company were fortunate enough to be able to arrive at Wadsley Bridge station, a short walk from the ground. The club trips had often brought with them victories and this one was no exception. However, the 2-0 victory had the gloss knocked off it when news arrived that Nottingham Forest had defeated Arsenal, leaving City still six points from safety.

Bob Whittingham

The following Saturday City threw everything at Newcastle United at Valley Parade. However, despite City's heroic endeavours the clinical finishing of the visitors ensured that once again City lost by a single goal. It caused one depressed player to comment 'we are the unluckiest team in the world!'

City's England international midfielder Evelyn Lintott was the inspiration behind a moral boosting victory over Sheffield United. It brought City to within four points of second bottom Bury. Striker Bob Whittingham suddenly found form with five

Mark Mellors

goals in three games and he began to repay his substantial transfer fee. The rejuvenated Bantams made their relegation rivals sit up and take notice when they visited second placed Everton, minus the injured Bob Campbell and Evelyn Lintott who was playing for England against Scotland. Bob Whittingham's goal gave City a surprise victory. However, the jubilation was short-lived when news of Bury's equally unlikely victory at Middlesbrough filtered through. It left City three points adrift, but form was on the up and they were now off the bottom.

Another of City's expensive signings also began to make an impact. Harold Hardman opened the scoring against bottom club Leicester Fosse, but within a minute the visitors had equalised.

Further goals from Frank O'Rourke and the now prolific Bob Whittingham gave City a vitally important 4-1 victory. Significantly for the club new goalkeeper Mark Mellors made his debut; his contribution was to prove absolutely critical in the coming weeks. When Preston North End were beaten two days later the great escape from relegation seemed more than possible. Even though defeat at Woolwich Arsenal left City needing to win all their remaining games to be certain of survival, when they defeated Chelsea 3-0 they had taken twelve points from a possible sixteen.

With the final two matches at Valley Parade the fans were confident for the first time in months that they could drag themselves out of the mire. When City found themselves two goals up at half-time against Notts County, morale was sky-high. However, in a calamitous second half George Chaplin first gave away an unnecessary penalty and five minutes later missed a challenge which let a County striker in one-on-one with Mellors. Suddenly a certain victory had been turned into a draw. Now City had to rely on others slipping up.

The final game of the season brought the FA Cup holders Manchester United to Valley Parade. United's neighbours, Manchester City had suffered a collapse in form and nerve, which left the Bantams knowing that victory would be enough to save themselves and relegate Manchester City. However, with two United players already promised a benefit match against their neighbours at the new Old Trafford ground that was poised to open its doors for the following season, there was no doubt that United would go all out for victory.

Frank O'Rourke gave City the lead, but United pushed City back and time and again Mark Mellors produced heroics between the sticks to keep the Bantams in the game. Fixtures against United had a history of being bad tempered affairs and this was to be no exception. City's tall keeper was badly bruised in a game that turned nasty on several occasions. City dished it out as well; James Comrie had to be cautioned by the referee for his 'robust' play. When six minutes of injury time was added it was too much for City president William Pollack. He was seen pacing the streets behind the Main Stand as time seemingly stood still. As the clock slowly ticked down the visitors subjected City's goal to a tremendous assault. They grimly hung on, but in the final seconds keeper Mark Mellors was knocked out as he saved a fearsome drive. He was literally propped up in the goal whilst City defended the resulting corner. It was scrambled clear and soon after relief came with the final whistle.

Thousands poured onto the pitch. The players raced for the dressing rooms but the bruised and battered Mellors was engulfed by jubilant fans. They carried him shoulder-high from the field. As the crowd gathered in front of the dressing rooms Frank O'Rourke and Evelyn Lintott appeared on the new balcony to huge cheers. Lintott had struggled to gain release from his teaching job in London to play in the match. The crowd remained for over an hour on the pitch. When City's international duo of Lintott and Hardman left the ground they were mobbed. They leapt onto a passing tram but scores of boisterous well wishers followed them onto the tram as it made a somewhat noisy journey into town. The players enjoyed a well-earned dinner at the Midland Hotel, where once again hundreds of fans stood in Cheapside singing and cheering the night away.

What an incredible escape it had been. Time and again City seemed to be down and out. Inspired by Peter O'Rourke, strengthened by the likes of Lintott, Whittingham and Chaplin they had not only dug themselves out of a seemingly impossible situation, they had laid the foundations for a period that was to prove to be the most glorious in the club's history. From the trauma of 1909 came the side that would take the club to the very summit of the English football.

BRADFORD CITY F.C. 1909-10.

[Photo]   [R. Scott, Manchester.

First Row—R. Torrance, M. Mellors, R. Campbell, and J. Duffy.

Second Row—P. O'Rourke (Sec. and Manager), E. H. Lintott, J. Murphy, G. Chaplin, W. P. Henderson, J. Comrie, J. McDonald, J. H. Spiers, C. Murray, H. P. Hardman, and D. Woods (Director).

Third Row—M. Spendiff, H. Peart, R. Whittingham, W. Clarke, F. O'Rourke, G. Handley, G. Robinson, P. Logan, and R. Bond.

Fourth Row—W. Grimes, J. Slemin, and W. Smith

Bradford City are a clever First League team. Colours: claret shirts, amber collars and cuffs, and white knickers. Their ground is situate at the Valley Parade, Manningham Lane. They were admitted to the Second Division of the English League in season 1903-04, and finished tenth from the top, with the following record; Played 34—won 12, lost 15, drawn 7; goals for, 45; goals against, 59, points, 31. The following year they were eighth from the top, and in 1905-06 they fell to the eleventh position. April, 1907, however, found them fifth on the list; whilst in 1907-8 they were champions of Division II, and thus secured promotion. So far they have done extremely well this season. (See next Saturday's "BOYS REALM"; giving further interesting particulars about Bradford City F.C.).

For a long and interesting article, giving further interesting particulars about Bradford City F.C.

Printed and published weekly by the Proprietors at 23, Bouverie Street, London, England. Subscription, 4s. 4d. per annum. Applications for Advertisement space should be addressed to the Manager, Carmelite House, Carmelite Street, E.C. Communications for the Editor should be addressed—"The Editor, THE BOYS' REALM FOOTBALL LIBRARY, 23, Bouverie Street, London, E.C." Agents for Australia: Gordon & Gotch, Melbourne, Sydney, Adelaide, Brisbane, and Wellington, N.Z. South Africa: The Central News Agency, Cape Town, Johannesburg, and branches. Saturday, December 25th, 1909.
N

CHAPTER TWO

Room at the Top

1909/10

Throughout the summer of 1909 the threat of a players' strike loomed large. A maximum wage of £4, set in 1901, roughly double the average working man's income, was still in place. Players were also bound to their clubs by the 'retain and transfer' system. Even after their contract expired, players could not be transferred without the consent of their previous club. The Players' Union (today the PFA) challenged the maximum wage and the transfer system. They also threatened to join the Trades Union Congress (TUC). As the dispute deepened, the Football Association withdrew its recognition of the Players' Union. A strike seemed inevitable, but on the eve of the new campaign a deal was struck where the Players' Union was once again recognised and bonus payments allowed.

The maximum wage was fairly widely supported. Writing in the *Bradford Daily Argus* under the pen name 'Preceptor' Fred Lintott claimed that the majority of players backed the maximum wage. Quoting the example of Scotland (where there was no maximum wage) two clubs, Rangers and Celtic, totally dominated the game. This was in complete contrast to the English league which was 'well balanced and not a single game can be regarded as a certain win for either side'.

As 'Preceptor' was the brother of City's England international midfielder and the future head of the Players' Union, Evelyn Lintott, we can take the remarks as being fairly accurate so far as the attitude of the players was concerned. What is interesting is why many Scottish players were attracted to the Football League with its maximum wage, whereas they could play in Scotland free of any such constraints. Undoubtedly, the English league had a much higher profile, and not every Scottish player had the opportunity to play for the Old Firm duo. However it does raise the question whether additional inducements were made away from the gaze of the club's accounts and the Football League?

Manchester was a hot bed of the Players' Union so the reaction of the crowd during City's opening game of the season at Manchester United was keenly anticipated. When the United players appeared on the field they were given an especially warm reception by the supporters which was perceived as an overt show of support for the Players' Union stance. Harry Hardman almost gave City an early lead when he beat two defenders and drew the keeper, only to see his shot cleared off the line. After that Martin Spendiff in the City goal was the busiest of the keepers and was largely responsible for the blank score line come the break. The second half was dominated by controversial offside decisions, or non-decisions, by referee Mr M'Que. United's Sam Blott was

Frank O'Rourke

thought to be at least five yards offside when he crossed for George Wall who opened the scoring with a low hard drive. City's Bob Whittingham and Frank O'Rourke were both adjudged offside when clean through on goal. Even United had time to feel aggrieved when Bannister was given offside just as he was about to shoot for a certain goal. To complete City's misery, in the dying minutes a deflected clearance fell at the feet of Frank O'Rourke and whilst an equaliser seemed a certainty, O'Rourke shot wide with the goal at his mercy.

A single goal defeat at the FA Cup holders was seen as a creditable start to the season. Optimism was high for the opening home game against Bristol City, the team beaten by Manchester United in the FA Cup final. The development of the side was reflected by the fact that of the eleven who lined up against Bristol City, only four had started the opening home game of the previous season. That great leader of men Jimmy Speirs had been signed from Clyde. A trio of Irish internationals, Harry Hampton, Jack Murphy and Jack Slemin also made their bow in the claret and amber. A new rule requiring keepers to wear different shirts to their outfield team mates meant that Martin Spendiff ran out in a royal blue top. Captain Evelyn Lintott won the toss and elected to play towards the Bradford End to take advantage of a stiff breeze. Dickie Bond and Frank O'Rourke teamed up to give City a two-goal lead within the first twenty minutes. Bond crossed for O'Rourke to bustle the ball over the line to put City one-up. A few minutes later, another Bond cross was met by the head of O'Rourke. The visiting keeper saved well, but Bond followed-up and eventually the ball came back to O'Rourke who shot City two up. The burly Scotsman completed a first half hat-trick as City cruised to a 3-1 victory.

The following Saturday City were involved in a goal feast at Bury. Bob Whittingham's late winner was said to be one of the finest ever scored by a City player. He showed tremendous close control, zigzagging towards goal, before unleashing an unstoppable shot that gave City a 4-3 victory. The goals kept coming during Spurs' first ever visit to Valley Parade. The front pairing of O'Rourke and Whittingham shared five goals, as the Londoners were demolished 5-1. City were simply irresistible. Jimmy Speirs was in dominant form and his passes had Spurs chasing shadows all afternoon. Physical presence was an essential part of the Edwardian game. During City's narrow victory over Notts County, Bob Whittingham attempted to take on the entire County defence. Incredibly, he threaded his way past six defenders, before being 'unceremoniously bowled over'. Appeals for a penalty were waved away. The *Bradford Daily Argus* was unsympathetic, commenting that 'Whittingham had practically asked for it by holding the ball so long'.

With City now in fourth position in the division the difficult trip to Newcastle was viewed with quiet confidence. However, Harry Hardman broke his wrist in a fall and City had to battle on with ten men. They went down to a single goal defeat, but the performance confirmed the growing belief that there would be no late battle against relegation this time around. City director Dr F Lindsay attended to Hardman's broken wrist. The amateur international would be out for several weeks and he returned to his Blackpool home to recuperate.

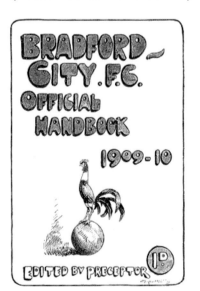

Apparently, the crowd at St James' Park wasn't as large as anticipated as Prime Minister Lloyd George was in town. As well as being able to hear the PM speak, there was the added attraction of potential trouble from Suffragettes. Indeed, several arrests were made during a bout of stone throwing. The defeat at Newcastle on 9 October was to be the first of three on the trot. At home to Liverpool George Chaplin twice made bad mistakes that allowed the visitors to take a two-goal lead against the run of play. Though City were overwhelmed at Aston Villa, the defeats didn't stop thirty thousand packing Valley Parade for the Yorkshire derby against Sheffield United. Harry Maskrey made his debut in

Valley Parade during its Edwardian heyday.

goal and kept a clean sheet as City got back to winning ways. The injury to Hardman gave an opportunity to youngster Peter Logan to show his worth. He quickly built up a formidable partnership with Jimmy Speirs on the left wing. Though they were in impressive form during City's victory at Woolwich Arsenal, it was City's right-winger Dickie Bond who scored the winner. In goal Harry Maskrey kept another clean sheet and he was to go five matches before he was finally beaten.

The visit of league leaders Blackburn Rovers attracted thirty-five thousand to Valley Parade to take on the in-form Bantams. Jimmy Speirs was a doubt as he was suffering from influenza and had a temperature of 101°F. Luckily for City, the plucky Scotsman declared himself fit. During the first half George Robinson's shot was deflected high into the air off a defender's boot. Rovers' keeper punched clear, but in doing so he tumbled over a crowd of players. With the keeper prone, Dickie Bond shot City into the lead. Peter Logan thought he had doubled the lead but he was adjudged offside as he shot into the net. When Chapman was sent off for Rovers in the second half, City began to dominate. Bob Whittingham saw one of his trademark thunderous drives rattle the crossbar before he scored the second and finished the contest. The local papers declared Bond and Logan to be the best wingers in the country, but once again it was Speirs who directed operations and his accurate passing kept the league leaders on the back foot all afternoon.

With City flying high in the table interest in the trip to Nottingham Forest on 4 December was intense. The Midland, Great Northern and Lancashire & Yorkshire railway companies laid on a total of five trains. Those travelling by the Great Northern were able to embark at Arkwright Street station only ten minutes from the ground. Heavy rain left two inches of mud on the pitch. Harry Maskrey was finally beaten in the Bradford City goal, but Bob Whittingham salvaged a point for the Bantams. At home to Sunderland the following Saturday another duck was broken. Within a minute of the kick-off Jimmy Speirs scored his first goal in English football. His volley from fifteen yards brought great applause confirming that Speirs had firmly established himself in the hearts of the City followers since he had arrived in the summer. Whittingham then scored either side of the break to give City a comfortable victory.

Christmas Day saw City demolish Middlesbrough 7-3 at Ayresome Park. Steve Bloomer had actually equalised for Middlesbrough three minutes into the second half, but from that point on City ran riot. Five goals in thirty minutes sent the one thousand Bradford City supporters in the ground wild with delight. Frank O'Rourke bagged a hat trick and Speirs a brace. Apparently City could have scored ten such was their dominance. The North Eastern Railway had organised an excursion from Forster Square which ran at full capacity. However four hundred people were left stranded in Bradford as the Midland Railway did not have permission from the North Eastern to run an additional excursion over that company's lines to reach Middlesbrough.

The return fixture on Boxing Day saw thirty-five and a half thousand jammed into Valley Parade. The gates were locked leaving hundreds outside. James Comrie brought down Boro's Steve Bloomer in the box to concede a first half penalty. Comrie made amends by scoring one of City's four in the second half as they once again swept Middlesbrough aside. The Bantams had scored twenty-five goals in just ten matches and were sitting proudly at the top of the first division at the turn of the year. It was tight but notwithstanding Bradford City were top of the Football League:

Division One 31 December, 1909

	Pl	W	D	L	F	A	Pts
1. Bradford City	19	12	3	4	43	22	27
2. Blackburn R	20	11	5	4	46	26	27
3. Sheffield Utd	21	11	5	5	43	24	27
4. Notts County	22	10	6	6	42	32	27

One notable departure from the club was the scorer of their first ever goal in the top flight, Willie Clarke. The 'dusky flier' had recovered from a lengthy injury, but such was Dickie Bond's form on the left wing that Clarke's chances of first team football were severely limited. Clarke left for Lincoln City on 31 December 1909.

Dickie Bond

New Year's Day 1910 brought the FA Cup holders Manchester United to Valley Parade. Striker Bob Whittingham had been playing for some weeks with a niggling ankle injury, so with the upcoming FA Cup tie in mind he was rested. Jimmy McDonald returned to the side, with Speirs switching wings to partner Dickie Bond on the right. The twenty-five thousand crowd (which was incidentally over twice the size of the attendance for the corresponding fixture at Manchester), had little to cheer as the two sides played out a tame contest on a mud bound pitch. Evelyn Lintott had a volley turned around the post and at the other end James Comrie nearly headed into his own net and only the timely intervention of Harry Maskrey saved the centre-half's blushes. In the second half Bob Campbell bowled over United's George Wall in the box and the winger gave the visitors the lead from the spot. City went down by two goals and it marked the start of a run of four league games when City failed to score. This sudden loss of form coincided with several injuries to key players. Nevertheless, it didn't stop criticism that the team 'was not trying' or worse had 'sold' some of the games. Captain Evelyn Lintott thought that the excellent start to the season had heightened expectations to unreasonable levels and he hoped that fans would accept that form does fluctuate throughout the course of a long campaign. The majority were still supportive of the team, but as ever a vocal minority were quick to pounce on any perceived failings.

The FA Cup first round tie against Notts County was switched to Valley Parade after City paid County £1,000. The City players went to Southport for special training, County to Skegness. In a complete reversal of today's priorities, the FA Cup took precedence over the league and players would often be rested in the run up to a cup game. Fifty men were employed to clear snow off the Valley Parade pitch and then protect it with fifty tons of straw. Despite the fact that admission prices had been doubled, excursion trains ran into Bradford from Carlisle, Morecambe and Sheffield. R. Gregson, one of the England selectors, was at the match to run his eye over Bond, Lintott and Whittingham. A muddy pitch spoiled the match and it wasn't until County's Jimmy Cantrell was sent off that City found form. They scored twice within ten minutes of the dismissal to take control of the tie. Dickie Bond did his England prospects no harm by scoring one of City's four goals. The policy of doubling admission prices came in for sustained criticism. Though the receipts of £969 were the second highest of the round, the attendance of seventeen thousand was well below the thirty-five and a half thousand and twenty-five thousand that had seen the previous two league matches at the ground. Though City were through to the next round, they were some £200 out of pocket.

Back in the league Bury visited Valley Parade on 22 January and found the pitch to be frozen hard. Forwards of both sides found it difficult to keep their footing on the treacherous pitch. The only real entertainment of the afternoon came when the ball became stuck in a trombone that was inexplicably lying alongside the pitch. Though the goalless draw gave City their first point of 1910, it did little to quell the growing disquiet on the terraces. However, a similar stalemate at Spurs the following Saturday was well received; in particular the sterling work of Maskrey, Campbell and Torrance in defence.

Once again the FA Cup brought with it heavy snowfall. The pitch was cleared but this time all the loose slush and sand was removed. It was said to be as flat as a billiard table, albeit almost devoid of grass. With prices at near normal levels twenty-eight thousand paid £1,336 to witness the tie with Blackburn Rovers. It was a tight affair, but the Rovers forwards always had the edge. Though Frank O'Rourke scored for City, the home forwards rarely found the space they needed and were well marshalled all afternoon. City lost 1-2 and O'Rourke suffered a knee injury that was to keep him out for three weeks.

Irish international Jack Slemin made his debut at Notts County and Speirs moved to centre forward to fill the shoes of the absent O'Rourke. Trips to Nottingham were always popular and four excursion trains were run. As the West Riding's pre-eminent club Bradford City attracted support from outside the city boundaries. Indeed one of the trains picked up at all stations on the Spen Valley line. It was a long day for all the trippers, as none of the trains departed Nottingham until after 11pm. Bob Whittingham was brought down in the box and he opened the scoring from the resulting penalty. Despite leading at the break the defence collapsed conceding three goals in fifteen minutes. Though Speirs pulled one back, it came too late and City went down 2-3.

Hopes were high that the dismal run would be ended when the Bantams visited bottom club Bolton Wanderers. In the event the 1-1 draw was seen as something of a triumph. City played the last fifteen minutes with nine men and two of those were carrying serious injuries. With only seven fit players City clung on despite a huge assault by Bolton. The dressing room looked like a hospital ward after the match. Slemin had been injured after a high-speed collision with the home keeper. Robinson had dried blood all over his face and shirt, as he had received several stitches to a head wound during the match. Chaplin carried on despite a nasty ankle injury. Lintott was so badly injured that the game was stopped as he received treatment. Lintott later commented that it was

Evelyn Lintott

the first time in his sixteen-year career that he had known a game to be halted for an injury! The City captain was one of those who battled on, despite being injured, and he was at the centre of the gallant stand of the final fifteen minutes. The injuries at Bolton resulted in major changes for the visit to Liverpool the following Saturday. The forward line was made up of reserves John Murphy and Arthur Rutter. Lintott's bravery in playing on at Bolton aggravated his injury to such an extent that he would be out for two months.

At Anfield a single goal defeat to a penalty was viewed as a remarkable effort given the circumstances. Evelyn Lintott was kept busy during his spell on the sidelines, as he was elected chairman of the Players' Union. He drew up a series of proposals: a rise in the maximum wage to £6 per week, fixed bonuses for results and a benefit match after five years service. He also looked at alterations to the widely disliked retention system whereby a player had to gain the consent of his previous club for a transfer, even if his contract had expired.

Full back Bob Campbell was yet another casualty ahead of the visit of league leaders Aston Villa to Valley Parade. He was replaced by Cleckheaton born Irvine Boocock. Villa spotted the potential weakness in City's defence and attempted to overwhelm the young debutant. Yet it was City who opened the strongest. Within two minutes they had a strong appeal for a penalty turned down. Jimmy Speirs, not a man given to wild comments, said that he had never seen a more clear case for a spot kick. Although City lost by the odd goal, the performance heartened the supporters. The youngsters being exposed at the highest level were fairing much better than expected.

A high scoring draw at home to Newcastle on 9 March was followed by a trip to Sheffield United. The game had been selected as the annual club trip and over a thousand made the short journey to Bramall Lane. The trips were seen as a lucky omen as they had never been beaten on those occasions. However, it looked bleak when Harry Maskrey allowed a weak shot to slip into the net. Once again City were fielding a weakened side, but O'Rourke gave the trippers heart when he equalised with a shot into the top corner of the net. Logan gave City their first league victory of 1910 with a shot from distance. It was a happy, and relieved, party that travelled back to Bradford that night.

That relief was short-lived. The visit of relegation haunted Arsenal to Valley Parade was described as 'a day in blunderland'. The City forwards were totally out of sorts and the Londoners gained a vital single goal victory. Two days later, 21 March 1910, Jimmy Speirs scored with a header whilst playing for the Anglo-Scots against the Home-Scots at Ibrox. The fact that Speirs had not appeared more often for Scotland was something of a mystery to the Valley Parade regulars. However, there was a perceived bias against Scots playing in England and despite the fact that the Anglo-Scots won 4-0 Speirs still didn't receive the expected call up.

It had been three long months since City had managed to win at Valley Parade, so victory over Sheffield Wednesday on 25 March was greeted with enormous relief. The omens didn't look good when Wednesday poured all over City in the first half. Fifteen minutes from time Frank O'Rourke scored from close range during a tremendous scramble in the box. Late in the game O'Rourke met a Logan cross and headed home to secure the long awaited victory at Valley Parade. The return match with Wednesday was played three days later. Bob Whittingham contrived to miss the train at Forster Square, despite being in the station. He followed on a later train but City were forced to start with ten men. Bob Torrance was pushed up to play as an emergency centre forward. Whittingham didn't appear at the ground until ten to four and by that time City were well on their way to a 1-2 defeat.

Dickie Bond's impressive form gained him a call up for England's game against Scotland at Hampden Park. It meant that he missed City's home game against another relegation-threatened London club, Chelsea. The winger was replaced by his brother Anthony Bond. After only two minutes another catastrophe seemed on the cards when Robinson ran across the flight of the ball un-sighting Maskrey and Chelsea had a shock lead. The visitors clung onto their lead, but in the final fifteen minutes City totally overwhelmed them and won 4-1.

Harold Hardman made a welcome return from injury at Blackburn Rovers on 9 April in what was his first game for five months. The match had a decidedly end of season feel about it. Dickie Bond was the only effective striker and even then he was starved of the ball. When he did receive a pass the home crowd cheered sarcastically. The goading of Bond got out of hand and such was the level of abuse that the referee stopped the match and, with the aid of several policemen, spoke to a section of the crowd.

The final three games of the season brought a defeat, a draw and a victory. It summed up the frustrating second half of the season. The mass of injuries had undoubtedly played their part. Though a seventh place finish was respectable by any standards, the fact that City had led the pack at the turn of the year, and had been in such fine form, caused one or two grumbles. However, the emergence of several young players gave great hope for the future. The likes of Robert Torrance and Peter Logan had established themselves as players of real quality. Their impact on the following season would prove to be enormous. As the players sat down to their end of season dinner at the Midland Hotel few could surely have envisaged the glories that lay ahead.

In 1910 the Football Association sought designs for a new FA Cup trophy. The previous trophy was being retired and would be presented to Lord Kinnaird in recognition of his services to the sport. The Bradford jewellers Fattorini's submitted the winning design. However whilst the new trophy was designed in Bradford a shortage of skilled silversmiths meant that the manufacturing of the trophy was sub-contracted to a Sheffield firm. This sub-contracting of prestige jobs was hardly new (in 1897 Fattorini's had designed the Rugby League Challenge Cup in Bradford and had the trophy made by a specialist firm in Manchester). The new FA Cup – Bradford designed but Sheffield made – was delivered in time for the 1910/11 season.

The Fattorini family had enjoyed a long association with Bradford City and their predecessors Manningham Rugby Club. Tony Fattorini had been Manningham's representative when the club become one of the founding members of the Rugby League in 1895. His brother, John Enrico Fattorini, had represented Bradford City in London when they applied for membership of the Football League in 1903. Finally Tony Fattorini's daughter had presented the club with a bantam mascot in 1909 and had thereby influenced the change of the club's nickname to 'the Bantams'.

Dickie Bond's England cap and shirt badge.

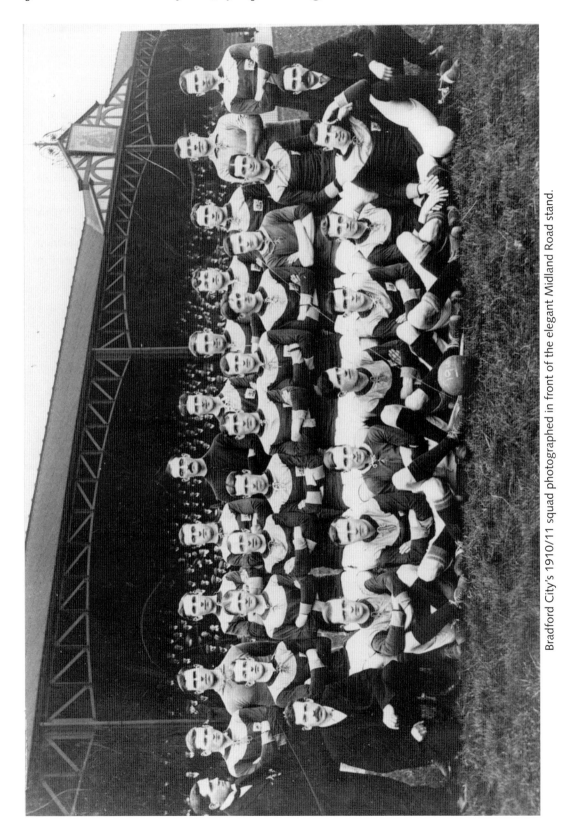

Bradford City's 1910/11 squad photographed in front of the elegant Midland Road stand.

CHAPTER THREE

Glorious 1911

1910/11

Archie Devine, David Taylor and Frank Thompson were signed during the summer of 1910 and would become regarded as a trio of significant signings. However, at first the patchy form of the previous campaign was in evidence. The first eight games brought three victories, three defeats and two draws. Jimmy Speirs' elevation to the captaincy coincided with a loss of form. Writing in the *Daily Argus* 'Milo' rejected criticism that the captaincy had effected Speirs' game noting that: 'The man who can follow the ups and downs of the rubber and oil markets – and make money out of it – is not the sort of fellow to be upset by the captaincy of a football team'. The response from the Scot was immediate. At Sheffield United he was back to his best, dictating a game City won when Frank O'Rourke met a Bond corner with a firm header ten minutes from time. Robert Torrance had been moved to centre half in place of the injured Hampton and was a revelation. His presence 'greatly strengthened the defence … his great advantage is his speed … never any question about his tackling ability.'

The great side of the era Aston Villa were early visitors to Valley Parade on 24 September 1910. City started strongly with Speirs rattling the crossbar from range. Two critical penalty claims went against the Bantams. First Speirs was knocked down from behind, then O'Rourke had his feet swept from under him. It was to be one of those days; Villa's winner was scored whilst virtually all the players had stopped expecting to hear the whistle for offside. The only man on the pitch who didn't hesitate was Villa's Walters who shot the ball home whilst standing two yards offside. The tough games kept coming. A trip to league leaders Sunderland saw David Taylor make his debut in place of the unfortunate Torrance. Archie Devine was rested at his own request as he was finding the transition from Scottish to English football tougher than expected. Jimmy Speirs equalised to give City a creditable point at Roker Park.

Glorious 1911

David Taylor opened the scoring with a header on his home debut against Arsenal. Once again City demonstrated their staying power by completely overwhelming the visitors in the last half an hour. Bond and O'Rourke scored to give the Bantams a three goal victory. A brace of defeats at the hands of Lancastrians Oldham and Blackburn, allied to injuries to Chaplin and Campbell, raised fears that the inconsistent form of the latter half of the previous season was about to repeat itself. Those fears

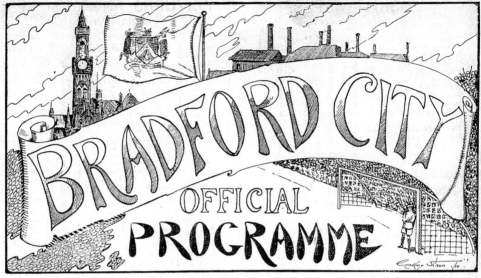

BRADFORD CITY
OFFICIAL
PROGRAMME

Published by the Bradford City Association Football Club (1908) Ltd., Burlington Terrace, Bradford.

VOL. 3, No. 5.]	SATURDAY, OCT. 29, 1910.	[ONE PENNY.

Jack Sharp is writing some interesting reminiscences in the " Football Evening News." Here is a good story which he tells :—

I remember a team travelling rather a long distance in a corridor carriage, in the other compartments of which were ordinary passengers.

I don't mention this because such travelling is in any way extraordinary, but because a certain player who was rather given to practical joking met with a startling lesson.

Somehow he got hold of a railway uniform coat and cap, and after putting them on, he quickly made his way to all the compartments and collected the tickets, shouting in stentorian tones, "All tickets, please."

When he returned to his own compartment there was, of course, much laughter, which suddenly died away when another member of the team snatched the bundle

of pasteboards and, apparently, threw them out of the window. Consternation was writ large upon the face of the joker, who had acted the part of collector, when he saw the tickets fluttering away down the line.

At the next stopping-place the real official collector came to do his duty, and as his unofficial forerunner was just starting to explain his joke and the outcome of it, the player who had, it was supposed, thrown the tickets out of the window reached forward and said, "Here you are, collector; I think you'll find them all correct !"

Upon which he handed over the bundle ; then turning to the practical joker he said, " Let that be a lesson to you, Jack, my boy ! Don't meddle with other people's duties ! The cards you saw fluttering in the breeze were an old bundle of tram tickets I had."

Programme cover from Bradford City v Nottingham Forest, October 1910 were blown away by five consecutive victories. The run began in unconvincing fashion when a reshuffled side had to come from behind to defeat Nottingham Forest at Valley Parade on 29 October. It was completely different at bottom club Manchester City, when the Bantams dominated. The emerging City hero Robert Torrance marked the former darling of Valley Parade Jimmy Conlin out of the match. Mark Mellors, in for the injured Maskrey, brilliantly saved a penalty and at last Archie Devine showed his shooting ability by hitting a brace.

Everton found themselves behind after only three minutes at Valley Parade on 12 November when O'Rourke scored in off the post. In a well-matched contest Everton soon equalised and Mellors had a busy time in the City goal. However, once again the benefit of Charlie Harper's training was shown when Everton tired in the final fifteen minutes and City scored twice through O'Rourke and Devine. A single goal victory at Sheffield Wednesday, where Bob Campbell returned to the team after a three week absence, was followed by a fifth victory when Bristol City were defeated.

Despite the great run the attendance at the Bristol City game was less than half of the previous home match. Bad weather, combined with a huge Unionist rally in the city, was to blame. Three Unionist candidates for the imminent General Election were all in the Main Stand to see O'Rourke shoot City into a fourth minute lead from outside the box. O'Rourke scored again, cleverly steering a Bond cross into the net with his knee and Speirs completed the scoring. With City fourth in the table and having won five consecutive matches the difficult trip to St James' Park on 3 December didn't seem too daunting. However, City crashed to their worst top flight defeat, losing 1-6. It was an inexplicable loss of form, though Newcastle were worthy winners, the margin of defeat caused consternation in Bradford.

The Bantams needed a change in fortune and got exactly that inside the first fifteen minutes of their home match against Spurs. Peter Logan raced to keep an over-hit pass in play and he just managed to cut the ball across the box. The Spurs keeper Tommy Lunn then seemingly had an easy task to gather the ball but somehow allowed the greasy leather to slip from his grasp and into the net. With Spurs tightly marking Bond and O'Rourke, it allowed Speirs and Logan to run riot on the opposite wing. Once again City's superior fitness told as the visitors were outplayed in the second half. O'Rourke and Speirs scored as City cruised to an easy victory.

As December progressed City went through a phase of winning one, then losing or drawing one. However, the defeats tended to be narrow affairs and nothing like the catastrophe of St James' Park. In the 2-3 defeat at Middlesbrough Speirs saw a goal disallowed after the home keeper scooped the ball back from behind the line. Of more concern the City captain was injured causing him to miss several games. He returned for the visit of Manchester United to Valley Parade on 27 December. The holiday match attracted thirty-eight thousand but one later arrival was the referee. His train didn't get into Bradford until half-time but fortunately there was a league linesman in the crowd, so a quick reshuffle of the officials saw the game start on time. Peter Logan scored for City after fifteen minutes with a cross shot from twenty-five yards. The missing referee appeared for the second half and seemed taken aback when the crowd broke out into a chorus of 'Hello Hello'. The official didn't know that this was the traditional welcome for the teams as they emerged from the dressing rooms and apparently he thought the crowd was being sarcastic at his late arrival! The second period saw United exert tremendous pressure on the home goal. It was almost a re-run of the 1909 match that City won to hang onto their top-flight status. Once again City denied United, though the visitors were convinced they had scored when Mellors wrapped himself around the ball during a tremendous goalmouth scramble. They claimed that the City keeper had pulled the ball back from over the line. The referee disagreed and awarded a free kick.

With the victory City were back up to fourth place. Although Liverpool visited Valley Parade a few days later and defeated City 1-3, the Bantams entered 1911 in great heart. The new year brought with it the FA Cup and dreams of glory in that prestigious competition.

Bury were the first visitors to Valley Parade in 1911. City were without Taylor, Torrance and Speirs but Frank O'Rourke won the game in bizarre circumstances. The ball came to him a yard off the ground but the centre-forward stooped to head. His header hit the post, came out, hit the keeper and went in via the same post. It was a valuable victory, but by now all eyes were on the FA Cup, which was viewed as far more important than the league.

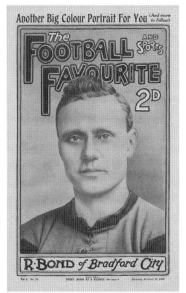

Another Big Colour Portrait For You *(And more to follow)*

The FOOTBALL AND SPORTS FAVOURITE 2D

R. BOND of Bradford City

The eventual FA Cup triumph began on a bitterly cold January day at New Brompton – better known today as Gillingham. City scrambled through by a single goal courtesy of Dickie Bond. The Crystal Palace must have seemed a million miles away as both teams struggled on a frost bound pitch. In the first half Mellors denied the home side with a brilliant save. City's only effort was a cross-shot by Speirs which was spilled by the home keeper with O'Rourke narrowly failing to intercept the loose ball. A few minutes after the break City were ahead. An early corner was not properly cleared and a second attempt to get the ball away fell to the feet of Bond. The winger's shot bounced across the frozen pitch and found the far corner through a crowd of bodies. New Brompton found City's defence implacable and only one effort five minutes from time caused any anxiety when Mellors tipped over a shot from the left. City were relieved to have got through on a tricky surface against opponents who fought hard to the last. There were flashes of good play from City, but they were few and far between.

Though City lost both of their league games between the cup games, they were still in sixth place and the Football League championship was a viable dream. However, the antics of England international winger Dickie Bond were attracting adverse headlines. After a wild night out in Otley, Bond was suspended by the City directors. Unfortunately, Bond then berated the directors in a local paper. A split with their star player seemed on the cards until Bond agreed to write a public apology and in return the club lifted his suspension.

Southern League Norwich City visited Valley Parade in the second round of the FA Cup. The Canaries had sensationally knocked out Sunderland 3-1 in the previous round, so while progress was expected thanks to the home draw, everyone knew that City would be in for a difficult battle. Three special trains from Norwich helped boost the crowd to twenty-seven thousand.

The game opened at a fast and furious pace. Mellors had to turn over a dangerous shot but City pressed forward and besieged the visitors' goal for fifteen minutes. However, on the half hour the Canaries took a shock lead, with Ingham heading past Mellors. City responded strongly, but both Speirs and O'Rourke failed to take good chances. The second period saw City encamped in the opposition half. Bond blasted over a Logan cross and a few minutes later Albert Kirkham nearly scored an own goal when clearing a hopeful punt from Campbell. The Canaries couldn't get the ball out of their own

BANTAM V. CANARY.

NIFFY—"It seems a pity when yer come ter think of it. Two fine birds like these and one of em's got ter die."

half, but doggedly they clung onto their one goal lead. Speirs drew out Bobby Beale in the Norwich goal, but Kirkham managed to race back to clear a near certain goal. However, Speirs wasn't to be denied for long. From a corner Robinson headed onto Speirs and he headed City level. City poured forward hunting for the lead. O'Rourke dribbled clean through, but was denied by the industrious Kirkham just as he shot. Ten minutes from time Beale failed to clear properly and Logan crashed the ball into the net. Right on time Norwich were appealing for a penalty when one of their forwards fell to the ground in a tangle with Campbell. To the relief of the majority of the crowd the referee waved away the appeals and City were through to the third round.

In the fortnight between the rounds City's league form slumped with a draw at bottom club Woolwich Arsenal and defeat at Oldham. City's ultra-defensive tactics at Arsenal incensed the home crowd who barracked Campbell for his hard tackling and Bond simply because he began to respond to the abuse. Eventually, Bond snapped and he was seen remonstrating with some of the crowd. After the game a few dressing room windows were broken and around two hundred spectators followed the City team to the railway station keeping up a torrent of abuse. The match at Oldham was played in a howling gale. Evelyn Lintott made his return following his lengthy injury and a side that had many changes from the cup team lost 0-1.

The third round of the FA Cup brought Grimsby Town to Valley Parade on 25 February 1911. Though Grimsby had been relegated out of the Football League and were competing in the Midland

Bob Torrance

League, they had beaten Croydon 3-0 and Crewe Alexandra 5-1 in the previous rounds away from home.

Peter O'Rourke made four changes from the team that had defeated Norwich. Chaplin, Hampton, Speirs and Peart made way for Torrance, Thompson, Taylor and Devine. Heavy showers had given way to bright sunshine, which left the ground very slippery. Six minutes before the interval City's Irish international Frank Thompson charged forward from the half way line. His initial

cross was cleared, but Thompson picked up the loose ball and swung the ball to Bond. The England winger then hammered a rising shot into the top corner to give City the lead. City continued to dominate the match, but during the second half they repeatedly wasted good opportunities. Thompson had a clear sight of goal but seemed to have wasted it when he switched the ball to his left foot. Although his shot was blatantly handled by John Arrowsmith in the box the referee ignored the protests. Later in the game the visitors finally put the City goal under pressure. A series of corners kept the twenty-five thousand crowd on edge, but Campbell and Torrance protected the City keeper so well that City keeper Mellors barely had to touch the ball. At the final whistle thousands of fans poured into the pitch. City were in the quarter-final of the FA Cup for the first time in their short history.

Trainer Charlie Harper had ten men under treatment in the wake of the cup-tie. Not surprisingly City were minus Campbell, Chaplin, Logan, Torrance and Speirs for the home game with Blackburn Rovers three days later. Despite the changes City won with a goal from Jimmy McIlvenny. It was the stand-in striker's third game for

Irvine Boocock

the club and all came between the cup ties. Speirs was back for the visit to Nottingham Forest on 4 March. Over seven thousand fans travelled to Nottingham as it was the annual club trip. They wore claret and amber hats and sported similarly coloured umbrellas. One supporter carried an FA Cup on a long pole. Bells, rattles and whistles had added to the din throughout the game and long into the night. Frank Thompson scored twice to the delight of the huge following that made up nearly half of the crowd. Once again City featured a much-changed side and Irvine Boocock and Billy Gildea both impressed whilst deputising for injuries.

As most of the supporters' trains didn't depart Nottingham until after 11pm the pubs did a roaring trade. Hundreds of pewter beer pots were stolen as things threatened to get out of hand. Copies of the *Yorkshire Sports* were sold on the streets of Nottingham and over eighteen hundred were eagerly snapped up by the trippers. One large party of supporters missed all the special trains and insisted on boarding a Scottish express. The logic was that the train had to pass through Shipley so at some point they would be able to get off. Unfortunately, the train's first stop was Carlisle and they had plenty of time to ponder their mistake in the early morning light of the border city!

Three days before the quarter-final star winger Dickie Bond was suspended for a month following the fracas at Arsenal. The Football Association upheld the suspension despite an appeal from City. Bond would miss the quarter and semi-finals. Peter Logan switched wings to replace Bond on the right. Second division Burnley were City's opponents in the quarter-final on 11 March 1911. They had defeated Exeter City, Barnsley and Coventry City all at home in the previous rounds. Chaplin and Torrance were unavailable for City but the popular captain Jimmy Speirs was back in the team.

Seventeen trains brought six thousand fans from Burnley. Interest in the match was such that specials were laid on from Barnsley, Chesterfield, Hawes, Leeds, Skipton, Sheffield and Rotherham.

ANOTHER STIFF CLIMB.

NIFFY : "Come on lad, if we get to the top of this we shall have a fair view of the Palace."

However, the vast majority of the crowd made a much shorter journey. They packed trams into town, walked several deep up Manningham Lane and overran the public houses en route. The Burnley fans poured out of the Exchange station and before midday the distinctive east Lancashire accent could be heard. One fan led an elephant on wheels around the city centre! The pubs and cafes did a roaring trade as the trippers were joined by thousands of Bradfordians in the early afternoon. Manningham Lane was a sea of humanity and lengthy queues formed at the turnstiles. Fully forty-five minutes before kick off the gates were closed with a recorded 39,146 spectators packing every inch of Valley Parade. The attendance remains Bradford City's record and represents the longest standing attendance record among the current 92 Premier and Football League clubs.

Shortly before kick off, hundreds of fans ran across the pitch from the Midland Road stand into the Main Stand. Others, tired from hours of crushing on the terraces, jumped over the fence and sat around the touchline. In the Midland Road side some fans climbed out of the heaving mass to wrap themselves around the ornate ironwork of the roof supports. A Burnley mascot in shirtsleeves ran around the touchline to ironic cheers and was pelted with orange peel and worse; he soon gave up his show of support for the safety of the stand.

Twenty-three minutes into the match, Speirs drew the Burnley defence out of position before passing to Logan on the wing. The Burnley goalkeeper Jerry Dawson and City's Irish international Thompson went for Logan's cross but Thompson got there first and headed City into the lead. After that both defences were on top. Logan should have put City two up in the second half but he shot wide with the goal at his mercy. At the final whistle thousands of fans invaded the pitch and crowded around City's triumphant players.

Three days later Manchester City visited Valley Parade. The former Bantams idol Jimmy Conlin was missing as he had been suspended by the Manchester club for a breach of discipline. In a game of terrible finishing City won 1-0 with a goal from stand-in striker John Young. All eyes were on the FA Cup. Indeed many players were rested and no chances were taken on even the slightest of knocks. At Everton the

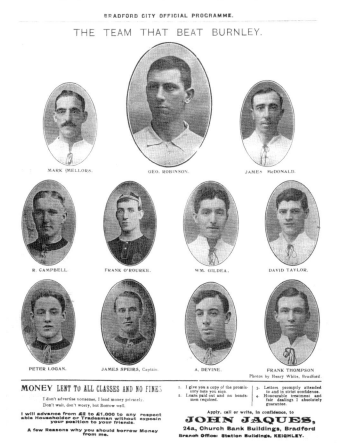

BRADFORD CITY OFFICIAL PROGRAMME.

THE TEAM THAT BEAT BURNLEY.

MARK MELLORS.   GEO. ROBINSON.   JAMES McDONALD.
R. CAMPBELL.   FRANK O'ROURKE.   WM. GILDEA.   DAVID TAYLOR.
PETER LOGAN.   JAMES SPEIRS, Captain.   A. DEVINE.   FRANK THOMPSON.
Photos by Henry White, Bradford.

Frank Thompson

week prior to the semi-final Bond, Gildea, Logan, Robinson, Speirs and Thompson were all absent. The makeshift side managed a creditable 0-0 draw at Goodison Park.

Though City had made the semi-final the national press were generally dismissive of their chances. They had yet to meet a first division side and the other three semi-finalists – Blackburn Rovers, Chelsea and Newcastle United – were deemed to be far superior to the defensively minded Bantams. The odds on City only lengthened when they were paired with five-time FA Cup winners Blackburn Rovers. However, City had beaten Blackburn at Valley Parade earlier in the season.

The semi-final was staged at Sheffield United's Bramall Lane ground on 25 March 1911. Seventeen trains carried a huge support to Sheffield. The City fans sported claret and amber umbrellas, teddy bears, bells, bugles and even a trombone! Arriving in Sheffield fairly early in the morning, the City fans paraded around in large gangs and they were reportedly 'a perfect blaze of claret and amber'. Many of the seats in the ground were taken up to three hours before kick off. The three-sided ground offered little protection from a bitterly cold wind. Only a rope separated the county cricket pitch from the football field. In these wide open spaces the thirty-six thousand crowd failed to match the frantic atmosphere of the quarter-final at Valley Parade.

Blackburn won the toss and elected to play with a gusty wind behind them. However, with Speirs and Devine playing deep, Rovers struggled to create many clear-cut chances. One fell their way when Mellors failed to gather a long shot. The ball bounced off the tall keeper's legs and fell to Rovers' Billy Davies only six yards out. However with the defence closing in, he made a mess

BRADFORD CITY OFFICIAL PROGRAMME.

THE CUP SEMI-FINAL TEAM.

Photo by Henry White, Bradford.

	MR. PETER O'ROURKE.	CAMPBELL.	MELLORS.	TAYLOR.
	ROBINSON.	GILDEA.	McDONALD.	
LOGAN.	SPEIRS.	O'ROURKE.	DEVINE.	THOMPSON.

Mark Mellors guards his goal during a Blackburn Rovers attack in the FA Cup Semi-final at Bramall Lane.

of shooting and the chance was gone. In the second period the game was turned on its head. An attempt to clear a corner failed and the ball fell to the feet of Frank O'Rourke who scored with a thunderous drive. Suddenly, City were all over their illustrious opponents. Playing a series of long sweeping passes, they continually had the Rovers defence in disarray. Archie Devine scored a second and City were on their way to the Crystal Palace. With snow now falling, some of the crowd left having seen enough. They missed, but probably heard, City's third, when Logan shot across the face of the goal and Thompson smashed a first-time shot into the net.

At the final whistle City skipper Jimmy Speirs was involved in an unseemly tussle for the match ball with one of the linesmen. Clutching the leather, Speirs joined his team mates at the Grand Hotel in the centre of Sheffield. So many toasts were proposed that one reporter had difficulty in remembering them! He wrote 'how we cheered and sang, and how hopefully we talked of that greatest triumph of all, a victory by the pleasant slopes of Sydenham!' When the team arrived back in Bradford shortly after ten o'clock they were met by thousands of well-wishers. The crowd stretched from the platform barrier out into Market Street. Some of the players escaped via the adjacent Midland Hotel, but Frank O'Rourke was carried shoulder-high down Market Street. As a result of the scramble for the ball at the end of the match three City players – Speirs, Thompson and Robinson – were censured by the Football Association.

Archie Devine

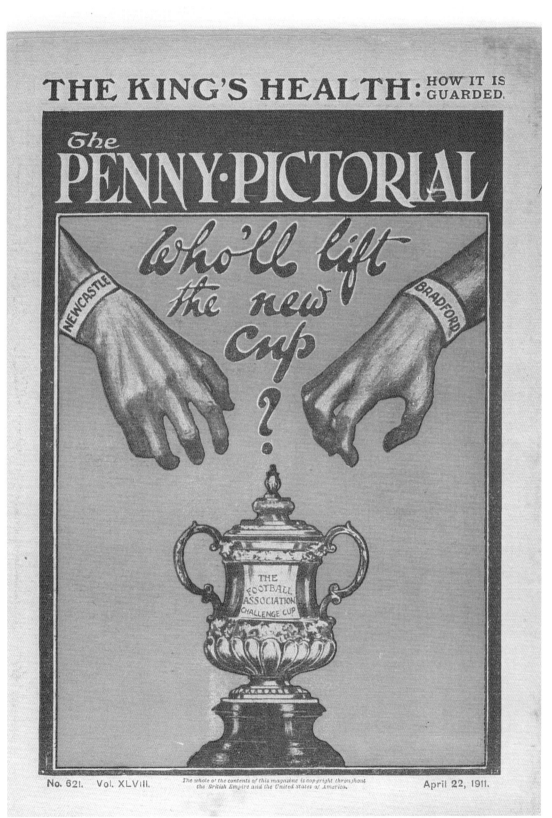

AN OPEN LETTER TO . . COLIN VEITCH, Newcastle.

My Dear Veitch,—It is with particular pleasure I offer you my congratulations on your fifth appearance in the Final tie. I know of no player who so thoroughly deserves the honour of leading his team, possibly to victory, on this great occasion.

It would be singular, after so many years, if you should again fail to lift the Pot at the Palace, for you are well aware you have yet to win a tie on that famous enclosure, only drawing there last year, and winning the replay.

I would recall to you how the despised Barnsley team last year almost defeated your dearest hopes, but I remember how wonderfully cool you were, always playing the game, leading your team on, confident in your ability to overcome the enemy.

Your men are skilled, not only in a playing sense, but what is far more important in a Final tie—*in tactics.* You won your last Final Tie by tactics when Barnsley were rushing you off your usual game by "get-there-at-any-price" methods. You saw the futility of pursuing your usual game, and you rushed and rushed to some purpose. It was that, and that only, which saved you the bitterness of a fourth defeat in the last six years.

In meeting Bradford City you are up against a stiff proposition, for their great victory over Blackburn Rovers proved them to be a team of more than average abilty. True, they have been lucky—and you yourself must admit your own good-fortune in this respect—in the draws, only being called upon to travel once, and that to a very poorly placed Southern League club, New Brompton, but they have done all that has been required of them, scoring eight goals to one during the process.

Popular fancy, undoubtedly, will make you favourites, but you will hardly want reminding that the odds are frequently upset.

I know you are not superstitious, and the fact that Old Moore has predicted that the Cup will be won by a club whose initial begins with a B will not disturb you.

I cannot say that this would be so with other footballers I know of. They are all more or less "nervy" and carry all sorts of ridiculous mascots to help them to victory. At all events, Bradford will do their best not to belie the prophet.

Colin, you are a deservedly popular player— few more so. As you are a schoolmaster by profession you are therefore well able to take care of yourself against the oft-repeated charge that players are simply hired ruffians. It is curious that Lintott —until lately captain of your opponents, but unfortunately laid aside with injuries—is also a schoolmaster.

Yours, etc.,
HERBERT BROGDEN.

AN OPEN LETTER TO . . J. N. SPIERS, Bradford.

Dear Spiers,—Bravo, Bradford! This must have been the cry of thousands of sportsmen all over the world when the news had been flashed abroad that you had been victorious over the famous Rovers of Blackburn.

Before the semi-final had been played you had been hanged, drawn, and quartered; you were said to have had not a ghost of a chance. Football scribes had, almost without exception, written of you in a rather sympathetic way, certainly not in a manner to give you any encouragement. "Beat the Rovers! Impossible. Simpson and Crompton will see to that!" But the glorious uncertainty of the winter game was never more exemplified than in this, your first semi-final.

The fact that, on the first occasion of reaching the semi-final, you pass also into the Final itself, is almost without precedent.

Joining Bradford only last season you must have soon gained the confidence of the directorate and your fellow-players.

I have always thought that of all players I have seen, perhaps with the possible exception of Bloomer, none saves his legs by using his head quite so much as you. You can, if you like, rough it with the best of them, twelve stone, but you prefer to make progress by skill coupled with elegance.

Now a word to you about this momentous match. You have at your command a team with at present a superior League record to that of your opponents. How has that success been attained? I venture to say by maintaining a high level of excellence.

Man for man you may not be so artistic, individually or collectively, as Newcastle, but I believe you are a shade faster, and this, together with your brilliant defence, may pull you through.

The man whom you are most likely to fear—to wit, Shepherd—will have opposed to him one of the greatest finds in League football to-day. In William Gildea—a player who, by the way, cost the club but a few pounds barely a couple of months ago—you have a centre-half spoken of as a second Thompson. I predict that he will play for Scotland in a very short time.

All lovers of football will welcome a win for you, for, like the sportsmen they are—of course, leaving out the biassed enthusiast—they love to see the honour go round.

It is no secret that your general secretary expects you to round off a fine season's work by bringing the new Bradford-made English Association Cup straight back to good old Bradford.

May good luck attend you!

Yours etc.,
FRANK YOUNG.

OFF TO THE PALACE.

NIFFY : " Return Tickets for Crystal Palace, please, for the Bradford City Players——all FIRST-CLASS."

The anticipation of appearing in the FA Cup Final initially gave City a huge lift. Eleven goals were scored in four successive victories. Archie Devine began the run with a brace from close range to defeat Bristol City. The players enjoyed their trip to the West Country, touring Fry's chocolate factory and taking cabs to the Clifton suspension bridge. The most remarkable victory came when Sheffield Wednesday were demolished 5-2 at Valley Parade. Wednesday had only conceded one goal in their previous eight games. The pick of the goals was a thunderbolt from Devine that the visiting keeper never even saw. Thirty thousand packed Valley Parade for Newcastle United's league visit; in effect it was a dress rehearsal of the cup final. Though the sides were much changed, 'Jock' Young's flying shot that curled into the top corner gave City a morale boost ahead of the big day. Young was at it again the following week as he hit two against Sunderland. Despite scoring eight goals in only nine games, Young didn't feature in any of the cup-ties. Star winger Dickie Bond had also returned to the side following his suspension, but Peter O'Rourke kept faith with his regular cup team and refused to be swayed, even by the availability of the England international.

As the final drew closer, City lost at Spurs and at home to Notts County. Quite naturally their attention was elsewhere. More worryingly, however, Bob Torrance broke down at Spurs with a knee injury.

Despite beating Newcastle United only fourteen days before the final, and being four places above their rivals in the league table, City were widely seen as the underdogs. Newcastle were the FA Cup holders and had been losing finalists in 1905, 1906 and 1908.

A staggering two hundred trains poured fans into London from all over the country. The Great Northern Railway, which served both Bradford and Newcastle, ran forty-three trains into King's

Telegraphic Address, "Parade, Bradford."   Tel. No. 2380.

Ground —
VALLEY PARADE.

Bradford City

Club Colours—
CLARET AND AMBER SHIRTS, WHITE KNICKERS.

Association Football Club (1908) Limited.

ENGLISH LEAGUE CHAMPIONS, II. DIVISION, 1907-8
. . Winners of . .
WEST YORKS. CUP, 1903-4, 1904-5, 1907-8, 1908-9.
WEST YORKS. LEAGUE. 1903-4, 1904-5.

. . Members of . .
THE FOOTBALL LEAGUE (Div. I.)
THE YORKSHIRE COMBINATION.

President and Chairman :
    W. N. POLLACK

Manager and Secretary :
    P. O'ROURKE

Registered Office :

55, Burlington Terrace,

Bradford.

RESERVES PARTY.

FRIDAY.

1-30 leave Bradford Midland Station
4-30 afternoon tea
6-10 arrive St. Pancras London
6-40 view Bedrooms and separate dining room reserved for this party
    at Midland Grand Hotel , St. Pancras
6-45 dinner in room separately reserved
7-45 leave for Oxford Music Hall by Taxi
11-0 leave Oxford Music Hall for Midland Grand Hotel
11-15 supper
12-0 bed

Saturday.

9-0 breakfast
10-0 drive to places of interest
12-45 luncheon at Midland Grand Hotel
1-45 drive to Crystal Palace
5-30 drive to Midland Grand Hotel
6-45 dinner at hotel
7-45 Tube to Alhambra

Note.

    This party will be in charge of David Menzies. The directors desire that until the Saturday evening this party will regard itself as entirely separate from the 15 players chosen to hold themselves in readiness for the match.

Itinerary of the reserve party

Bradford City's official party photographed prior to departing Bradford Forster Square
en route to the FA Cup final.

Cross. Twenty trains, including one conveying the City team, ran into St Pancras on the Midland Railway. City had something of a special relationship with the Midland, not least because the company leased Valley Parade to the club. The Midland Railway Company's carriage works in Manningham made a silver horseshoe, which they presented to the team. A large crowd gathered to witness the departure of the official party, including the fifteen players from whom the team would be selected, as they left Forster Square at half past three on the afternoon of Friday 21 April 1911. Driver Luck, who had driven the team's train to the semi-final, was once again at the controls as the train pulled away from Forster Square, past Valley Parade and towards the distant capital. The great invasion of London had commenced a few hours earlier with the departure of the reserve team from Forster Square.

Eleven trains conveying some six thousand City fans followed in their wake. The streets of Bradford were busy all through the night. Streams of supporters made their way to Forster Square and Exchange stations. Along the route vendors sold claret and amber 'favours' that trippers placed in their lapels or attached to hats. As each train started, cheers went up and the fans began singing the popular City song 'Hello Hello' which echoed down the platforms as the trains departed into the night. The first train disgorged its bleary-eyed travellers onto the capital's streets at half past four in the morning!

The first team party arrived at St Pancras at quarter past eight in the evening. Waiting at the hotel for the team was a good luck horseshoe, sent by the men of Bradford's Tramways. The team visited the Euston Empire Theatre, a short walk from their base at the Midland Railway's fabulous St Pancras Hotel. Given the huge number of fans of both clubs arriving at St Pancras and the adjacent King's Cross in the early hours, it may not have just been pre-match nerves that kept the City players awake in their hotel rooms above the great station.

The day of the match, Saturday 22 April 1911, saw the players enjoying a drive to Hyde Park before they departed to the final venue – the Crystal Palace. Then, as now, cup finals had a reputation of being disappointing games and the 1911 final proved to be no exception.

On a rock hard pitch the game fizzled out into a goalless stalemate. City repeated their tactics

THE ILLUSTRATED SPORTING AND DRAMATIC NEWS.

THE F.A. CUP FINAL AT CRYSTAL PALACE. — NEWCASTLE UNITED DRAW WITH BRADFORD CITY

1. *Newcastle forwards attacking.—A centre from Wilson.*   2. *A good save by Mellors, the Bradford goalkeeper.*   3. *Campbell, Bradford's "solid" back.*

Bradford coming out.   *The Bradford goalkeeper saves at the cost of a corner.*   *A stand among the trees.*

Glorious 1911 and Bradford City's Golden Age

The Captain's toss-up prior to kick-off

from the semi-final of keeping the game tight in the first period. It was fully twenty minutes before the first shot worthy of note was recorded. Newcastle's George Wilson shot low but Mark Mellors made a reaction save with his left foot. After that, with City's midfield dropping deeper and deeper, Newcastle struggled to get beyond the resolute City defence. Initially, City were a side transformed after the break. A poor header from Billy McCracken almost let Frank O'Rourke in but after a wild scramble Newcastle cleared their lines. Peter Logan found Jimmy Speirs with a cross and the City captain flashed a shot inches over the bar with the Newcastle keeper Jim Lawrence completely beaten. For the first time the Valley Parade 'Hello' chorus was heard. However, a bad slip by David Taylor let George Jobey get clean away and from that moment City seemed to lose confidence. With the Bantams back in their defensive shell the match reverted to a stalemate and before the end some in the sixty-eight thousand crowd began to drift away.

The final scenes in the act were played out at King's Cross and St.Pancras. From eleven that night both stations were besieged by fans from both clubs. Though some had hours to wait before their train was due to depart, the stations and the streets around them became a magnet. Some slept where they could, others sang and even danced. The nearby pubs were packed to suffocation and stalls did a roaring trade in food and drink. It was 3am before the area had any semblance of peace. Train after train pulled away with their loads of weary travellers heading for the north and home.

Back in Bradford thousands had gathered outside the offices of the evening papers in Market Street whilst the match was being played. The Town Hall clock was forever consulted as the minutes ticked by. A shout went up 'City's scored', but either a practical joker or wishful thinking was at work. Eventually, news of the scoreless draw emerged and the crowd melted away. The team arrived back at Forster Square at quarter to six on the Sunday evening. Thousands waited to cheer them as they left the station but with everyone's minds on the replay, it was a mere interlude and the players quickly dispersed for their respective homes.

The replay took place on Wednesday 26 April 1911 at the virtually brand new Old Trafford ground. It was by far the biggest game ever staged in Manchester and applications for seat reservations came from Portsmouth, Cardiff, Aberdeen and Bristol. The Lancashire and Yorkshire Railway Company organised five special trains from Bradford Exchange calling at Bowling Junction, Low Moor and Halifax. Manchester Corporation laid on trams to Old Trafford from the Cathedral, less than a two-minute walk from Manchester Victoria station. The Great Northern Railway Company ran an excursion direct to the Old Trafford station. The train departed Thornton at 11.35am and called at Queensbury, Clayton, Great Horton, Manchester Road, Bradford Exchange and Dudley Hill. The only station it didn't call at en route was Horton Park, the station

Bradford City defending at the Crystal Palace

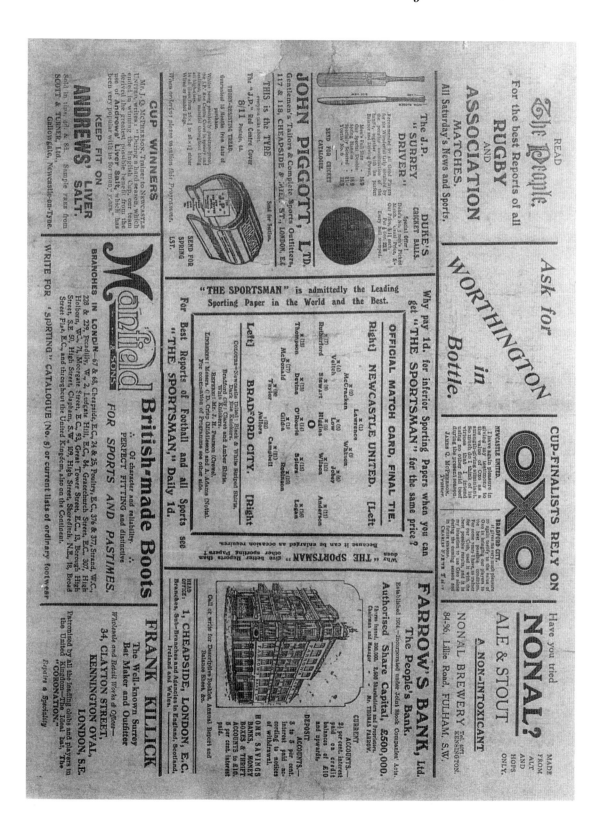

that served Bradford (Park Avenue) FC's ground! City's favoured railway company, the Midland, ran one train on a roundabout route to Manchester from Forster Square via Manningham, Shipley, Bingley, Keighley and Earby.

Old Trafford was overwhelmed. Forty minutes before kick off the gates were closed with over thirty thousand people locked out. In complete contrast to the bright sun and hard pitch of the match at the Crystal Palace, a boisterous wind blew around the ground and the pitch was soft after heavy rainfall the previous day. Newcastle won the toss and elected to play with the wind. With the elements with them, they adopted a shoot on sight policy. Newcastle captain Colin Veitch shot narrowly wide and Mark Mellors had to concede a corner whilst saving a dipping drive from Wilson. Newcastle had five corners before City could launch a meaningful attack. However, nerves were affecting both sides and twice Whitson kicked into touch rather than take on City winger Peter Logan. Gradually, City eased themselves into the match and from a George Robinson free kick they found themselves ahead.

Robinson found Frank Thompson and the Irish international ran into space and shot. Colin Veitch attempted an overhead kick and accidently caught Thompson's head, as result of which the City winger collapsed in a heap. Jim Lawrence in the Newcastle goal failed to punch clear whilst seemingly distracted by the incident and as the burly figure of Frank O'Rourke closed in, Jimmy Speirs headed the ball over the keeper's shoulder and into the net.

Newcastle redoubled their efforts in an attempt to equalise whilst they still had the advantage of the wind at their backs. Robert Torrance was a Trojan in the City defence; the auburn-haired Scotsman was everywhere, time and again denying the Magpies much vaunted forward line. Twice Veitch shot narrowly wide, but at the half-time interval City's lead was still intact.

In the second half City had the lion's share of the play and should have extended their lead. However, it was Newcastle who came closest to scoring when Alex Higgins saw his shot punched out by Mellors. Higgins followed up, but Mellors saved his second attempt. However, the two collided with such force that both had to receive treatment before play could resume. With the wind at their backs City began to make good use of their trademark sweeping passes. George

Jimmy Speirs, extreme right, heads the winning goal of the Cup Final replay at Old Trafford.

Mark Mellors cuts out a cross in the FA Cup Final replay at Old Trafford

Robinson grazed the crossbar with a long-range effort and moments later Peter Logan saw a similar effort go agonisingly close. In a late raid Mellors once again had to receive treatment when he crashed into the onrushing Veitch. However, it proved to be Newcastle's final attempt to rescue the game. City resumed their attacks and shots from Speirs, Torrance and Logan all went close. In the end Speirs' first half header proved to be enough and at the whistle thousands of City fans poured onto the pitch in celebration.

Jimmy Speirs led his team up to receive the FA Cup from Charles Crump, vice-president of the Football Association. The cheering crowd, which had by now completely filled the pitch, made speeches impossible. But Crump was heard to tell Speirs that as it was the first time the new trophy had been played for, whoever might win it in the future, Bradford City's name would be the first on the trophy. The team arrived back in Bradford at 9pm to be greeted by huge crowds outside the Exchange Station. Captain and goal scorer Jimmy Speirs held the FA Cup trophy aloft to deafening cheers. The Thackley and Idle Brass Band tried in vain to make themselves heard such was the noise. It was estimated that a hundred thousand people were on the streets to catch a glimpse of the cup winners - if so that would have been equivalent to nearly a third of the entire population of the city. What a moment it must have been as the players struggled to cross town to a celebration dinner at the Midland Hotel. This truly was the city of Bradford's finest hour.

Amazingly, City played Middlesbrough at Valley Parade the very next day. A penalty, taken by the unlikely figure of full back Bob Campbell, settled the match. The season was completed at Preston North End on 29 April. The pitch was a mud bath and not surprisingly, after four games in eight days, the players' hearts weren't in it. They lost 0-2 and the momentous season was over. City finished in fifth place. Although they were actually on the same points as the third and fourth placed sides an inferior goal difference pushed them down two places. At the end of the 1910/11 season Bradford City supporters could reflect on the fact that their club was holding its own among the traditional elite of English football. Not only had City secured the FA Cup but sat alongside Manchester United (champions), Aston Villa (runners-up), Sunderland (3rd), Everton (4th) and Sheffield Wednesday (6th) at the top of the Football League.

TWO LEADING SOCCER FOOTBALL TEAMS OF THE SEASON—
1910—11.

BRADFORD CITY CUP TEAM.

[Photo by R. SCOTT & CO., Manchester.

P. O'Rourke (Sec.),   Robinson,   Campbell,   Mellors,   Taylor,   Harper (Trainer),
    Bond,   Spiers,   O'Rourke,   Devine,   Thompson,
    Logan,   Gildea,   McDonald.

MANCHESTER UNITED FOOTBALL TEAM.—Champions of the First League, 1910—11.

[Photo by CHAMBERS & CO., Manchester.

    Green,   Halse,   A. Nuttall,   J. Nuttall,   J. Broad,
Bacon   Meredith, Hodge,   Stacey,   Whalley,   Holden,   Moger,   Stanford,   Turnbull,   Magnell
(Trainer),   Homer,   Connor,   C. Roberts,   West,   Bell,   Linksen,   (Sec.),
    Aspinall,   Sheldon,   Donelly.

36

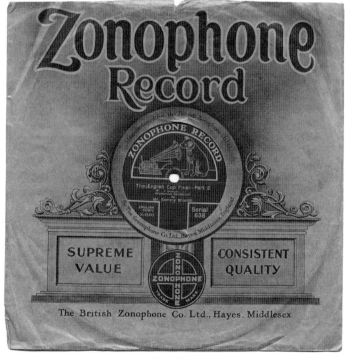

A huge range of memorabilia was produced in the wake of City's FA Cup victory.
Even a century ago there was good money to be made from the Cup winners.

CHAPTER FOUR

The Defence of the Cup

1911/12

The opening game of the 1911/12 season saw Aston Villa at a sweltering Valley Parade. Although the twenty-five thousand crowd witnessed City enjoy most of the possession, Villa led at the break. Just two minutes into the second half Thompson's cross was controlled instantly by Speirs, who then equalised from close range. Bond skimmed the bar and Speirs was inches wide as City sensed a winner. Tempers boiled over when Villa's Bache ran into Speirs. The referee and a linesman had to get between the two players and the crowd was said to be 'fairly aroused' by the incident. Speirs played O'Rourke in down the centre. He scrambled past two opponents and shot low into the corner of the net. City were rampant. Centre half Bob Torrance went on a mazy run that caught the Villa defence napping. After beating several opponents his shot hit the inside of the right post, ran along the line and back into play. It was academic as City ran out fairly comfortable 2-1 winners.

The fixture list was tough on City as it was none other than Newcastle United away in the second game of the season on 9 September 1911. It gave the Magpie's an almost instant chance to avenge the cup final defeat. Roared on by a forty thousand crowd the home side hit the bar and Torrance had to clear off the line in a lively opening. City defended manfully and somehow kept the scores blank in a half totally dominated by the home side. Once again during the second half City were a side transformed. Fifteen minutes in, Thompson crossed and Speirs shot into the corner of the net. The City captain then combined with Bond but this time his shot flashed narrowly wide. Thompson had an effort tipped over the bar before Speirs put the result beyond doubt with his second of the match.

Sheffield United visited Valley Parade to test the cup holders' 100% start to the season. City took the lead in controversial circumstances. Dickie Bond was flagged offside as he raced down the wing. However, the referee overruled the decision, Bond's

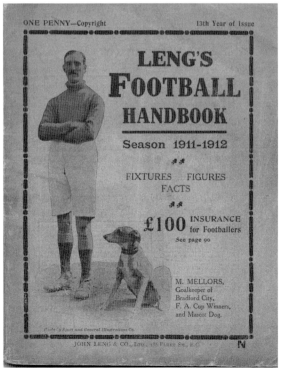

cross was handled and much to the Blades disgust a penalty was awarded. After protests the referee consulted his linesman and following a lengthy discussion the penalty award was allowed to stand. Bond made no mistake from the spot shooting high into the net. In the second half City's passing went astray and the visitors did a lot of attacking. In the dying seconds it seemed an equaliser was a certainty when George Gane in the City net fell to the ground leaving United's Charles with an open goal. As he shot Gane stuck up a leg and diverted the ball wide of the gaping goal. After three victories from three games City stood proudly at the top of the Division One. Across the city Bradford (Park Avenue) FC were second in Division Two. It was quite a weekend for the city of Bradford.

Only six minutes into the game at Oldham Speirs badly twisted his knee trying to keep the ball in play. He switched to the wing and tried to play on but he could barely hobble. Oldham were one up at the break and Speirs didn't appear until the second half was well underway. When Oldham scored a second Speirs wisely retired. The City captain was to be out for weeks. He had fluid drained from his knee, but the joint had been badly wrenched and the cartilage displaced. It was the first time the club had been beaten with the cup final defence on the field. Bob Campbell said: 'Well, it shows we can be beaten after all. Really, I didn't think we could'.

City bounced back immediately with a single goal victory over Bolton Wanderers. A gale was blowing over the Spion Kop and the players found the ball difficult to control. In the second half

George Robinson

Oscar Fox's cross eluded several players before arriving at the feet of Peter Logan. He was tackled as he shaped to shoot but the ball spun to Jimmy McDonald who scored with a low shot into the corner of the net. Dickie Bond hit the bar but McDonald's goal was enough to ensure victory.

At Preston the following week City quickly found themselves two goals behind and in serious trouble. However, Peter Logan pulled one back and with their usual strong second half City were soon back in the game. Logan saw a shot tipped onto the bar; the ball shot straight up into the air but it came straight down into the hands of the relieved keeper. Logan then had both his legs swept from under him in the box. Both he and Dickie Bond chased the referee up the field, but their protests were ignored. However the equaliser wasn't long in coming and Frank O'Rourke scored in a mad scramble.

In light of Dickie Bond's suspension following his exchanges with the crowd at Arsenal the previous season, the volatile winger was rested for the return trip to London on 14 October. Mark Mellors in the City goal became the target of the Arsenal fans and he was bombarded with apple cores throughout the match. Arsenal only had one shot on target from open play throughout the entire match. Notwithstanding, that shot and a penalty was enough to condemn City to a two goal defeat.

The mini-slump was halted in spectacular fashion when Manchester City were swept aside at Valley Parade. In pouring rain Frank Thompson gave City the lead on thirty minutes when he beat his marker and clipped the ball past the on rushing Gus Beeby in the Manchester City net. The visiting keeper intercepted a Bond cross but two City players challenged him and the ball fell free to Frank O'Rourke who passed the ball into the empty net. Dickie Bond joined in the fun, beating two men and shooting City three up. Irvine Thornley pulled one back for the visitors but Robinson headed City's fourth from a corner and the rout was complete. The victory put City back on top of the table.

The Bantams luck was out at Goodison Park. Dickie Bond missed 'the chance of a lifetime' and

Frank O'Rourke hit the bar with such force that the ball rebounded twenty yards back up the field. Everton scored with a tap in at the far post and, despite appeals for offside, it was enough to secure the points. West Bromwich Albion, who had been vying with City for top spot all season, visited Valley Parade on 4 November 1911. Though the sides were level at the break, City's goal had some fortune attached to it as James Blair's shot cannoned off a defender into the net. The traditional strong second-half showing was then enough to see City home. Frank O'Rourke held off three defenders to allow Frank Thompson to score into an open net to give City the lead. Blair hit his second with a shot into the top corner and Thompson also scored his second with a shot that hit a post, rolled over the line and back into play. Fortunately, the eagle-eyed officials realised that the ball had crossed the line and for the second consecutive home game City had scored four times.

At Roker Park on 11 November 1911 Blair gave City the lead with the first attack of the match. Although Charlie Buchan equalised with a shot in off the bar shortly afterwards, the draw was overshadowed by an ongoing feud between Frank O'Rourke and the Sunderland keeper Scott. During the second half O'Rourke charged into Scott. The pair indulged in a barging match until the whistle went. O'Rourke waved his fist in the goalkeeper's face and Scott threw the ball into O'Rourke's face in retaliation. Later O'Rourke was clean through, but couldn't control the bouncing ball and Scott collected. After the ball was cleared O'Rourke said something to Scott. The keeper was incensed and only the timely intervention of players from both sides stopped another fight breaking out.

David Taylor

The burly O'Rourke continued his war on keepers the following Saturday when he bundled over the Blackburn custodian at Valley Parade. Blair tapped the ball into the empty goal but the referee awarded a free kick. O'Rourke had the last laugh when he scored five minutes from time to send the thirty-five thousand strong crowd wild with delight. Despite the rough and tumble the game was said to have been 'one of the best played on the City ground'. The victory allowed City to leapfrog Blackburn into second place, one point behind the leaders Newcastle United.

David Taylor became the first of the cup-winning side to leave Valley Parade when he transferred to Burnley on 1 December for a large fee. Apparently, his wife had never taken to life in Bradford and Taylor himself disliked the city. He was at Valley Parade for barely a year; however, in that time City changed him from a forward to a top class defender. He made fifty-one appearances for the Bantams, but only seven months after the cup final he left for Turf Moor. He was destined to win the FA Cup again with the Clarets in 1914.

With injuries mounting City's form collapsed and over the Christmas period the club used seventeen different players in three games. In fact, reserve goalkeeper Martin Spendiff made his first appearance since 1909. In nine league games between Boxing Day 1911 and 2 March 1912 City scored a mere three goals. Thankfully, the defence did their bit conceding only six in same period. There were some creditable results, such as the goalless draw at Aston Villa on 30 December. Frank Thompson nearly made it a memorable victory with a weakened team, but in the final minute he hit the bar with the home keeper stranded.

Peter O'Rouke went scouting in Ireland and came back with Irish amateur international keeper Fred McKee. He went straight from the boat at Holyhead and into the match at Liverpool on New Years Day 1912. The debutant did well as City's makeshift team had to play with ten men when Frank Thompson was injured. They lost by a single goal but emerged with much credit. Winter weather then gripped the country and severely disrupted the fixture list. A home game against

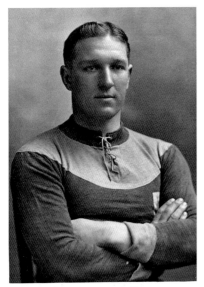

Bob Campbell

Newcastle United was played in a snowstorm. The weather was so bad that there was a mass pitch invasion as supporters fled from the open Spion Kop to the cover of the Midland Road. Six minutes into the second half the game had to be abandoned. Bob Torrance commented that they 'would have been better if they had been wearing corned beef tins instead of boots'.

The defence of the FA Cup took City to Queens Park Rangers in the first round. The cup holders were seriously handicapped when Frank O'Rourke received a bad injury to his right ankle. He moved across to the wing, but he could barely run. At half-time the tough Scotsman did not take his boot off fearing that his ankle would swell up and prevent him putting his boot back on. He put the injured foot, and boot, in a bucket of hot water. City played for, and got, a scoreless draw. It was an inauspicious start, but they were still in the cup competition.

The scheduled replay was called off when the Valley Parade pitch practically ended up under water following a hefty downpour. It was rescheduled for a 2.15pm kick-off on Thursday 18 January 1912. Snow was cleared off the pitch, but a light covering was left and the lines marked out in red. Snow fell throughout the game which was scoreless at the break. In the second half Harold Walden had his legs swept from under him in the box and, after a consultation with the linesman, the referee awarded City a penalty. However, after Dickie Bond had placed the ball on the spot, the referee changed his mind and resumed play with a dropped ball. City were not to be denied for long though. Thirteen minutes after the break the QPR keeper spilled the ball and Walden dribbled around the stranded keeper and tapped it into the empty net. On the hour Walden got between the central defenders, drew the keeper and shot home. Suddenly, City were all over the visitors. Peter Logan got clean through and shot between the keepers legs to put City three up. Just before time Walden got his third and City's fourth.

The terrible weather continued and the league game against Sheffield United was abandoned thanks to a combination of fog, heavy rain and rapidly melting snow. One of City's most popular players, full back Bob Campbell, had his benefit match against Oldham Athletic. Unfortunately, he was unable to play due to a severe cold and neuralgia. He attended the match, but was confined to the stand. A large board was carried around the ground thanking the crowd for their support and expressing Campbell's regret that he couldn't play. His team mates presented him with a case of four pipes and some fishing tackle. Oscar Fox was injured in the first half and had to retire. He returned, but was limping and played out wide. His valiant effort was in vain and Fox had to retire before half-time with the game scoreless. At the break Speirs, Torrance and Logan walked around the pitch with collecting sheets and over eight hundred pounds was collected from the twenty-five thousand crowd. The game ended in a stalemate and City were left in eighth place in the table.

Chelsea were the visitors to Valley Parade for the FA Cup second round on 3 February 1912. Frank Thompson was out and Louis Bookman – City's Lithuanian-born Irish international - made his debut. Chelsea had been in special training at Broadstairs on the Kent coast. They arrived in Bradford on the Friday evening before the match. The snow still covered the pitch and it had been deliberately left in place to protect the surface from the frost. Salt was used to mark out the pitch and the black lines stood out vividly against the white snow. The lines were said to have looked like they had been drawn by a giant fountain pen – black ink on a white cloth. The teams ran out in bright sunshine, but it was bitterly cold. Chelsea's former City striker Bob Whittingham was given a special cheer when he appeared (he had left Valley Parade in April 1910 after scoring 31 goals in just 49 appearances for City). Within two minutes City were ahead. Chelsea's Cameron mis-kicked which allowed Bond a chance and the England winger hammered the ball into the top corner and City were on their way. The conditions were treacherous. Players found it difficult to keep their footing and Chelsea's left winger Billy Bridgeman fell heavily following a collision with City's strapping full back Bob Campbell. The Chelsea man broke his finger and was in terrible pain as his bone was left protruding from his skin. Peter Logan then scored City's second. Chelsea made little headway with Bob Torrance keeping Bob Whittingham quiet on his return to Valley Parade.

Back in the league, City were without Frank Thompson for the visit of Preston North End as Thompson was away on international duty with Ireland. Joe McCall's shot for North End deflected off Torrance's boot and flew past a stranded Mellors to give Preston a single goal victory. To compound a bad day, Thompson returned injured from his international sojourn. At Bolton the following Saturday another deflection put City in arrears. Just eight minutes from time the ball looped off Joe Hargreaves leaving Martin Spendiff as stranded as his team mate Mellors had been in the previous match. A minute from time Bolton added a second and City were facing a slump in form. It was six games since they had scored in the league.

Archie Devine missed Arsenal's visit to Valley Parade on 17 February as a result of a pulled muscle. Durham-born John Clark was handed an immediate debut having signed from Bathgate. After twenty-eight minutes Walden scored City's first league goal for ten hours. In a frantic goal mouth scramble the Irish sergeant-major poked the ball home to huge delight. The fans had almost despaired of seeing another league goal. Bond had to leave the field after receiving a bad kick from Peart. The referee cautioned the Arsenal man and Bond was able to resume after five minutes of treatment. Arsenal eventually equalized, leaving City without a league win in seven matches. However, the draw had been achieved without eight first choice players: Mellors, Robinson, Torrance, Speirs, Logan, O'Rourke, Devine and Thompson. The mass of injuries was taking its toll on the league form and it was widely acknowledged that City would have been favourites to retain the cup had it not been for the absentees.

In the FA Cup third round Bradford received its dream tie – Bradford (PA) v Bradford City. It was the first real meeting of the two Bradford sides since the Park Avenue club had switched codes from rugby in 1907. The city was in ferment in the days leading up to the tie. The *Yorkshire Observer* printed one hundred thousand 'favours' adorned with the colours of the two clubs. On the morning of the match, 24 February 1912, queues began to form along Horton Park Avenue. By kick off nearly twenty-five thousand were crammed into Park Avenue and several thousand were turned away. Fans clambered into trees and up telegraph poles in an attempt to witness the game. The centre of Bradford was almost devoid of males, although a fair crowd gathered in Town Hall Square with their eyes riveted to a score indicator provided by a local sports outfitters.

At Park Avenue a huge cheer filled the air when the claret and amber jerseys appeared in front of the "Dolls' House" – then another as the green and white hoops of Bradford (Park Avenue) followed. It was the first season that Bradford had worn green and white in preference to the club's traditional red, amber and black. The change had been introduced by Bradford's new Glaswegian manager, Tom Maley who had encouraged the adoption of Celtic's colours.

Frank O'Rourke

Bradford City. 1912.

The Bradford City team photographed at Oakwell, Barnsley,
prior to the scoreless FA Cup quarter-final of 1912

After thirteen minutes Frank O'Rourke scored for City with a cross-shot at the Horton Park End. Bradford's woes continued when their full back Watson retired after taking two heavy knocks. In those days before substitutes Bradford (Park Avenue) had to play over half the match with ten men. Both sides came close to scoring, especially City through Dickie Bond near the end. However O'Rourke's goal was enough to settle the first Wool City derby. After the game Horton Park Avenue was a sea of humanity. Trams, packed inside and out, could only travel at walking pace through the throng.

Bob Campbell was absent for the league match at home to Everton. However, Jimmy Speirs was back after nearly six months injured. City's luck seemed to be out again when O'Rourke hit the bar but there was Logan to score from the rebound and City were one up at the break. City attacked like men possessed. Torrance was everywhere, centre-half, midfield and up front - he was said to be 'all over the shop'. The woodwork was struck three times but City at last ended their league hoodoo by winning for the first time in eight games.

Bradford City's reward for their victory over Bradford was a quarter-final tie against Barnsley at Oakwell. It ended in a goalless draw, Irvine Boocock broke his ankle in the last minute. He had to be carried back to the station on the back of keeper Martin Spendiff. City were expected to easily defeat Barnsley in the replay at Valley Parade. Many Barnsley fans were reported to have cycled to Bradford to witness the match. With the talisman Speirs missing with a rib injury, another stalemate ensued. An altercation between Mellors and Barnsley's George Lillycrop resulted in the tall City keeper aiming a kick at his opponent. An enraged fan ran on the pitch and had to be escorted from the ground by the police. Both sides were said to be overeager. A quarter of an hour of extra time was played during which Mellors collided with the post after making a great save. He collapsed after trying to stand up and was off the field for seven long minutes receiving treatment. Still the sides could not be separated and a third match was needed.

The second replay was played at Elland Road, Leeds but the ground was totally unsuited for such a big match and the facilities were overwhelmed. Over thirty-five thousand paid at the gate. One turnstile was broken down, another robbed of its takings and thousands got in without paying. Barnsley played much of the game with ten men after Leavey suffered a broken leg having collided with City's Hampton. Half-time had to be extended to twenty-five minutes due to the encroachment of the crowd onto the pitch. The second half was another stalemate. Before extra time could be played the game was abandoned as the police struggled to keep thousands of fans

Postcard produced in Barnsley prior to the FA Cup quarter-final against Bradford City.

off the pitch. It was estimated that around seventy thousand people were inside and outside the ground during the match.

The two teams tried again on 21 March 1912, this time at Bramall Lane, Sheffield. At last the stalemate was broken: Barnsley took the lead after fifteen minutes and led at the break. In the second period Frank Thompson slipped with an open goal at his mercy. However, Speirs equalised from a corner and Devine put City 2-1 ahead twenty-six minutes into the second period. It was a frantic match. Barnsley hit the woodwork twice and City struck it three times. In one mad moment Barnsley hit the City bar, City broke away and Frank Thompson hit the Barnsley bar! Walden then missed a glorious chance to finish the tie but amazingly missed from three yards. The semi-finals were seconds away when Barnsley's Lillycrop scored with the last kick of the match. Extra-time was even more frenetic. But, just when it seemed that yet another replay would be needed, Barnsley again scored right on the whistle. There was no time for City to reply and the cup holders were knocked out. Seven hours had been played. It was an astonishing cup-tie and one that must be almost unequalled in the long history of the FA Cup. Barnsley went onto the win the cup that year so at least the trophy remained in Yorkshire.

Just two days after the epic cup-tie City were back in league action at Blackburn Rovers. A decision was made to rest the entire team who had played at Bramall Lane forty-eight hours previously. The resulting 1-3 defeat at Ewood Park was seen as reasonable in the circumstances. Another depleted and half-fit team lost 0-4 at Manchester City, but due to City's cup exploits there was no let up as the fixtures piled up on top of one another. Sheffield Wednesday's visit to Valley Parade on 30 March saw the visitors arriving at 3.15pm due to having been stranded at Penistone as a result of the railways being disrupted by a long running miners' strike.

Peter Logan

45

Glorious 1911 and Bradford City's Golden Age

Jimmy McDonald

The reliance of the country on coal during that period was immense. Bradford still had its own mining district and the strike was solid at Drighlington, Tong, Low Moor and Wyke. A knock-on effect saw the pressure of the town gas halved as the production of gas relied on the supply of coke. The shortage of coal also resulted in six hundred dye workers being laid off with another two hundred working a one or two day week. In West Bowling, where a thin seam of coal existed near the surface, hundreds began digging to supplement dwindling supplies. A sixty-five year old man died when one ad hoc mine collapsed in a disused quarry at Rooley Lane. All across the city soup kitchens were set up to help feed families.

The match against Wednesday at least offered a welcome distraction from the travails of district. City started brightly and after only six minutes Jimmy Speirs tapped home the opening goal following good work out wide by Peter Logan. Speirs was running the show and his incisive passing picked out Oscar Fox just after the half hour. City's Sheffield-born striker dribbled past his marker Worrall and beat the keeper from an oblique angle. A few minutes later Speirs shot was parried by Davison in the Wednesday net with the ball returning to Speirs who smashed it hard and low for City's third. Just before the break the visitors shot over but inexplicably the referee awarded a corner kick and from it Wednesday scored via a deflection off Jimmy McDonald. Speirs was in sensational form and completely dominated the game from inside-left. The Sheffield press wondered how Barnsley would have dealt with the Speirs-Logan combination had Logan been played out wide as he did against Wednesday. Bradford City were comfortable 5-1 victors and Speirs bagged a hat trick. Sadly, the widespread hardship caused by the miners' strike kept the attendance down to a mere nine thousand, significantly less than the forty thousand who had witnessed the Boxing Day match against Manchester United at Valley Parade.

The following Saturday brought a change of fortune. As the *Bradford Daily Argus* put it, 'after the Lord Mayor's show comes the dustcart' to describe City 0-2 defeat at bottom club Bury. In a wild gale both Bury goals came from corners. Things looked even gloomier when relegation haunted Liverpool visited a rain lashed Valley Parade two days later. Dickie Bond blazed a penalty over the bar just after the half hour. Liverpool's Speakman made City pay for the miss by putting the visitors ahead with a shot that went in off the underside of the bar. After the break Liverpool survived several loud appeals for penalties and Peter Logan missed when one-on-one with the visitors' keeper. On the hour Martin Spendiff completely missed a cross leaving Gilligan with the simple task of tapping into an empty net and giving Liverpool a vital two points in their battle against the drop. There was time for Logan to whip a cross in a yard from goal only for a host of City players to miss the inviting ball.

The following day City met Newcastle United at Valley Parade in a re-arranged match. Frank O'Rourke was in the thick of it from the off, hitting the post with a header early on. Then the burly Scotsman clattered into United's keeper Lawrence. The ball rolled free after the collision but just as O'Rourke was about to shoot into the empty net the Magpie's McCracken appeared from nowhere to clear. On the hour the visitors took the lead following good work from Wilson and Peart, which resulted in Hibbert scoring with a shot. Fifteen minutes from time Dickie Bond's cross came back to him and the England winger brought City level despite appeals for offside. City took a point but their record since the turn of the year, when they were considered as one of the favourites to win the championship, had been dismal. Fourteen games had seen only three victories as the Bantams took just nine points from a possible twenty-eight. A lengthy injury list, fatigue caused by the epic FA Cup ties and a fixture backlog were to blame for the slump.

The penultimate home match of the season brought Middlesbrough to Valley Parade on 13 April 1912. The weather was said to be 'more suited to a walk over the moors or a bicycle trip'. Many, still short of money following the miners' strike (that had only ended twelve days earlier) stayed away and the crowd was eight thousand down on the Newcastle game. However, one cannot ignore the fact that City had played three home games in five days. Quite obviously with many workers still suffering from the effects of the prolonged miners' strike, the free charms of the moors and country lanes took preference over a first division fixture with nothing at stake. Harold Walden was quick out of the blocks, charging down a casual clearance by Williamson in the 'Boro' goal in the first few seconds of the match. Unfortunately for City's amateur international the ball bounced agonisingly wide of the gaping goal. On the quarter hour City were awarded a penalty but once again Bond shot wide – it was the third consecutive penalty the Bantams had missed. City's woes were compounded when the Boro keeper clawed a Jimmy McDonald shot out of the top corner. Astonishingly the referee awarded a goal kick. The official ignored his linesman who was flagging vigorously for a corner. City's luck finally changed in the thirty eighth minute when Bond played a gently weighted pass into the path of Walden who fired the ball home. Walden added a second and City had a precious victory to celebrate.

Missing from the side was Frank Thompson who was on international duty. He partnered Bradford's McCandless as Ireland defeated Wales 2-0 at Cardiff. The Park Avenue man hit both goals. The match must surely have been the only time Bradford supplied two international strikers for the same country?

The Irish connection continued as City, despite a heavy fixture list, departed for a mini tour of Ireland. The tour started in Belfast, a city in mourning as its pride, the Belfast-built Titanic had sunk just a few days earlier. City returned to play a re-arranged match against the beaten FA Cup finalists West Bromwich Albion at The Hawthorns ground. Archie Devine struck the post as City gained a creditable draw and then played their final game of the season – another re-arranged match – at home to Tottenham Hotspur the day after the trip to West Bromwich. There was a collection for the Titanic Disaster Fund prior to the game. City topped off the season with a three goal victory over Spurs. Harold Walden celebrated his call up for the British Olympic side with a hat trick, one of which was a penalty - no doubt scored to the relief of the City fans after the trio of penalty misses in previous matches! Walden was to win a gold medal for Britain in the Olympics in Sweden. He was far from being the only amateur plying his trade in the Football League; other clubs represented were Birmingham City, Chelsea, Derby County, Hull City and Portsmouth.

The FA Cup triumph of the previous season was commemorated on 26 April 1912 when a cot and brass plaque was unveiled at Bradford Infirmary. The £500 cot had been provided as a lasting memorial to the cup triumph. Though as City director Thomas Payton wryly noted 'if the sixty-thousand people who received them when they came home with the cup had subscribed 2d each the amount would have been at once raised. It only showed the poverty of the enthusiasm of football followers when they were asked to put their hands in their pockets'. City found themselves further out of pocket when they were fined £150 for fielding weakened teams. Cup winners Barnsley were fined £100 and the losing finalists West Brom £150. Clubs were entitled to compensation if a League match was cancelled due to their opponents playing in FA Cup ties. Due to City's epic involvement they had an astonishing £1,000 claimed against them. Fortunately the Football League committee dismissed most of the claims.

In May City's balance sheet was published showing a profit of £1,218. The club's AGM at the Mechanics Institute heard that the defeat against Barnsley in the FA Cup quarter final had hit the finances. An appearance in the semi-final or even final would have probably seen the

Jock Ewart

47

club's debts of £1,405 wiped out. The combination of a bad winter and the miners' strike had hit attendances. Despite the lower than expected income it didn't stop the club securing the services of Scottish international keeper Jock Ewart, though City's chairman William Pollack admitted the fee paid for Ewart was 'not much to his liking'. A shareholder commenting on the large sums spent on players' wages, travelling expenses and refreshments, wondered how the club would have fared had they been knocked out of the FA Cup in the first round? It was a telling comment and one that has resonance with today's obsession with playing and progressing in the Champions League. It gives us both a valuable insight into the fragility of the club's finances and the importance of the FA Cup in both prestige and financial terms – quite clearly the Football League Championship came second to the FA Cup.

Bradfod City 1912/13

CHAPTER FIVE

The Colour of Money

1912/13

The new season started in the toughest possible fashion with a trip to Villa Park. During the summer Aston Villa had spent around six thousand pounds on four players. The *Bradford Daily Argus* reflected that Villa's spending over the summer was 'almost equal to a whole season's revenue of some of the lowly league clubs'. The ability of a handful of wealthy clubs – notably Aston Villa, Everton and Newcastle United – to dominate the transfer market was causing concern. The unpredictability of the league was often referred to as one of its greatest assets. Publically at least there seems to have been a consensus that buying success was somehow distasteful. Bradford City tapped into the rich seam of Scottish talent for reinforcements and John Wyllie made his debut in the Bantams' defence. The burly Scot was at times overwhelmed by the quick first time passing of the Villa forwards and it was later acknowledged that it was probably a mistake to hand him his first division debut against what was widely acknowledged as the best attacking force in the country. However, Wyllie was not the only defender to struggle as City went down to a 1-3 opening day defeat.

The first home match of the season brought Liverpool to Bradford on 14 September; they had a remarkable record of never having lost at Valley Parade. Peter O'Rourke made three changes to the side mauled at Villa Park: Mark Mellors returned in goal in place of Jock Ewart; George Gane replaced Irvine Boocock; and the fit again Robert Torrance ousted John Wyllie in the centre of defence. The changes seemed to have worked when Peter Logan's early corner was deflected off Jimmy Speirs to Harry Walden who scored with a fast shot. Archie Devine nearly doubled City's lead but his fierce drive struck the Liverpool defender Bob Pursell full in the face, knocking him to the ground to the amusement of some of the spectators. After a quarter of an hour Dickie Bond and Jimmy Speirs exchanged passes before Speirs scored from a narrow angle to the delight of the twenty thousand crowd. Though Liverpool recovered from the early blitz, there was no further scoring and City had their first victory of the campaign. Robert Torrance, George Robinson and Jimmy McDonald dominated their opponents. Torrance was picked out with special praise in the *Bradford Daily Argus*: 'As a despoiler he was supreme. He fairly bottled up the Liverpool inside forwards by his clever tackling and super-abundant energy'.

In mid-September 1912 the Football League announced it was consulting with clubs regarding the inequalities caused by players' benefit matches. There was strong support across the game for such matches. Eligible players, with either long or exceptional service at a club had a normal league fixture selected for their benefit and received the gate receipts. Of course clubs with large supports could tempt players to sign for them with the promise of a lucrative benefit match. The disparities were illustrated when Manchester United's Billy Meredith received two thousand pounds for his benefit match, whereas John (also known as 'Jack') Sutcliffe at Plymouth Argyle pocketed a paltry £15.

Although Meredith was one of the stars of the age, Sutcliffe had an interesting sporting pedigree. Born at Shibden near Halifax, Sutcliffe had played rugby union for Bradford and Heckmondwike and had made one England international appearance before he was suspended from rugby union for professionalism. He changed sports and joined Bolton Wanderers as a forward but switched to goalkeeper where he made 364 appearances for the Trotters. He also won five England caps, played for Millwall, Manchester United and finally Plymouth Argyle. After retiring he became coach at Southend United and Vitesse Arnhem. Sutcliffe eventually returned to his native Yorkshire after the Great War and became Bradford City's trainer. A conviction for beating his wife soured his reputation as a great sportsman and he died in relative obscurity in Bradford in 1947. Of course, all that was to come in 1912 and the point being made was that the promise of a lucrative benefit could undermine the maximum wage in that players would be attracted to the clubs with the largest attendances.

Bradford City had paid over sixteen hundred pounds from gate receipts for benefits to Peter O'Rourke, George Robinson, Jimmy Millar and Bob Campbell and that amount was likely to increase. It was noted that Newcastle United could pay a benefit of £2,000 whereas Notts County would struggle to raise £500. Players were aware of their growing influence but in late September, 1912 Aston Villa's Chris Buckley overstepped the mark when he demanded £250 to re-sign for Villa in addition to a benefit of £450. The Football Association fined Buckley £24 and suspended him until 30 April, 1914. Villa were fined twenty-five guineas for continuing to pay Buckley when he had not re-signed for the club. The stiff suspension imposed on Buckley was undoubtedly designed to send out an uncompromising message to the players. Villa's fine by comparison was almost insignificant. The authorities were either content, or felt compelled, to turn a blind eye to the complicity of the clubs and especially one of the standing of Aston Villa. Although the players were beginning to understand that their star status gave them bargaining power, the clubs were still very firmly in control and it would take another half century before the balance of power would shift.

In Football League competition, Bradford City (without the injured Speirs) lost 0-2 at Bolton Wanderers on 21 September, 1912. Goalkeeper Mark Mellors was severely handicapped in the game having been knocked to the ground by a Bolton forward in the third minute and shortly afterwards received a violent blow to his thigh. The Bantams' woes were compounded by off the field disciplinary problems when Bob Campbell returned to his native Scotland without permission after being told he would not be selected for the trip to Bolton. Although he reappeared in Bradford the same weekend he failed to attend a training session and was suspended by the club as a result.

Campbell was missing for over a week and was therefore out of the side that faced Sheffield United in a gale at Valley Parade on 28 September. On the quarter hour a long clearance by the Blades full back Benson was picked up by the wind and Jock Ewart, in the City goal, was caught in no-man's land. The ball bounced over his head and left the visitors' forward Leafe with an open goal. However, it proved impossible to control and Leafe punched the ball into the net. The referee, stranded at the other end of the pitch, was forced to consult both linesmen before he disallowed the goal. City took the lead after Jimmy McDonald was fouled following a great piece of skill that took him clear of several defenders. The lead was increased when John Wyllie, back in the side following his tough debut at Villa, crossed for Archie Devine to score. Sheffield United narrowed the score with a second half penalty but Bradford City hung on to record a 2-1 victory.

The absence of City goals in the second period against Sheffield United was a disappointment for those who had taken advantage of the newly applied half price admission for those entering the ground at half time. The reduced admission was a recognition of the fact that virtually everyone worked Saturday mornings prior to the Great War and some could therefore be delayed by work commitments and may have been unable to make the 2pm kick-offs. Of course some supporters may have also been 'delayed' in nearby public houses as pubs could open when they pleased prior to 1914.

The Newcastle United legend Jock Rutherford chose the visit of the Bantams to St James' Park for his benefit match. The national standing of Bradford City is illustrated by the large number of benefit matches they were chosen for at away games and as recent FA Cup winners they were a genuine attraction to crowds all around the country. Bob Campbell had reappeared and travelled with the team as Bob Torrance was suffering from a cold. In the event Torrance played and Campbell continued his largely self-enforced absence from the team. City started brightly and thought they had taken the lead when Dickie Bond's shot flew into the net via the underside of the crossbar. However, the linesman's flag was raised for offside. City forward Jimmy McIlvenny twisted his knee and was forced to play out of position in the defence. He handled the ball in the box when no one was within yards of him and Newcastle took the lead from the resulting penalty. McIlvenny retired hurt a few minutes later and Bradford City were forced to play a counter-attacking game. The *Bradford Daily Argus* reported that Harold Walden played Dickie Bond in with a long accurate pass and City's international winger went 'after it like a shot from a gun'. He placed the ball past the outstretched hand of Lawrence in the Magpie's goal and it went into the net off the far post which was said to be 'a glorious goal'. It gained City a hard earned point and extended their unbeaten run against Newcastle United to six games – quite a feat against arguably the greatest team of the Edwardian era.

The hugely popular Frank O'Rourke – Bradford City's all time leading goalscorer until Bobby Campbell overtook his tally in the 1980s - chose Oldham Athletic's visit to Valley Parade as his

benefit game on 12 October, 1912. Thick fog caused one of the linesmen to miss his connection as the conditions played havoc with the railway timetable. As it turned out a replacement linesman was in the ground and the players took to the field in a thick haze. When Frank O'Rourke appeared the Idle and Thackley brass band struck up 'Auld Lang Syne'. Unfortunately for the Scottish striker the anticipated attendance was reduced by the fog but over twenty thousand paying spectators and a collection raised £531 19s 9d. After the match (a forgettable scoreless draw) the club's directors presented O'Rourke with a silver cigarette case.

Bradford City's erratic start to the season continued when they completely outplayed Chelsea at Stamford Bridge. Jimmy Speirs was on form and would continually draw opponents before passing to his fellow strikers Harry Walden and Peter Logan. The former opened the scoring but fittingly it was the dominant Speirs who scored the second. Oscar Fox beat two men and shot against the post before Logan gathered the rebound before passing to Speirs who shot into the net. At the other end Bob Torrance kept City's former striker Bob Whittingham quiet. The Bradford City goal had a miraculous escape when Jock Ewart palmed Ormiston's header onto the underside of the bar. City's Scottish international goalkeeper then threw himself clear of the falling ball which bounced up off the line for Ewart to parry it away. The referee waved play on as the Chelsea players, and the home crowd, appealed for a goal. Reportedly for ten minutes after the incident the crowd jeered the referee and Ewart and the game was played at a furious pace. Fortunately Dickie Bond took the heat out of the contest by scoring City's third.

Thick fog and drizzle welcomed Woolwich Arsenal to

COPE'S
"CLIPS"
CIGARETTES

No. 152—CHAPLIN
Bradford City

Noted Footballers

George Chaplin

Valley Parade on 26 October. City decided to play in their change all white strip but they had to change back to claret and amber when it was realised the white clashed with Arsenal's colours. After a minor delay the game got underway. The inclement weather kept thousands at home and the attendance of seven thousand was fifteen thousand down on the previous home match. The fog affected attendances all across the north: only eight thousand at Derby, five at Manchester City, ten at Everton and fifteen at Newcastle United. The *Bradford Daily Argus* reported: 'The players flitted about in the hazy atmosphere like ghosts and it was difficult for spectators to follow the play'. After only seven minutes Dickie Bond cleverly eluded his marker and crossed for Jimmy Speirs to score with an easy header. Banks of fog swept in and out of the ground and on several occasions play was completely obscured. Bond continually slipped past his markers and outpaced the Arsenal defence. Speirs and Harry Walden took full advantage and gave City a comfortable 3-1 victory.

The two fine victories attracted twenty two thousand to Valley Parade for the visit of Sunderland on 2 November. The optimism was soon punctured and City found themselves behind after only seven minutes and two down at the break. Oscar Fox gave the large home crowd hope when he raced into space between the visiting centre backs and scored with a fine shot high into the net. Dickie Bond was then inches away from an equaliser. In the last seven minutes the Bantams completely capitulated and conceded three goals. The 1-5 defeat was their heaviest at home in their first division history. The supporters must have been perplexed by City's performances. The following Saturday they travelled to Manchester City who had conceded only one goal at home all season and the Bantams were three goals ahead inside fifteen minutes. Oscar Fox opened the scoring with a 'brilliant' left foot shot and Jimmy Speirs struck twice to give City an unassailable lead. When Speirs gave City a one goal lead with a header early in the next game

against West Bromwich Albion at Valley Parade, the supporters must have been thinking that the Sunderland debacle had been firmly put behind them. Unfortunately an unlucky goal drew the visitors level just before the break: Jock Ewart lost the ball in a crowd of players and a resulting shot hit Bob Torrance and deflected into the empty net. It ended 1-1.

In midweek George Chaplin's benefit match - a friendly against Bradford (Park Avenue) - attracted a large crowd to Valley Parade. On thirteen minutes a familiar routine outwitted the visitors when Dickie Bond beat Blackham and crossed for Jimmy Speirs to score with a header. Bradford had a chance when they were awarded an indirect free kick just outside the penalty area. As Scott ran up the players in the Bradford City wall deliberately moved to give him a clear sight of goal. Jock Ewart stood as though he was going to try and save the shot but stepped aside at the last moment to allow the ball to enter the unguarded net. Some visiting supporters

Irvine Boocock

thought they had equalised but the laughter from the crowd quickly made them realise that Scott had been duped to kick the indirect free kick direct into the net and so the 'goal' was disallowed. Immediately after the restart Frank Thompson scored with an unstoppable thirty-yard drive and City won the friendly 2-0. After the match both teams were presented with commemorative gold medals by George Pauling, the prospective Unionist candidate for Bradford Central on the balcony overlooking the pitch. The two teams and directors then retired for tea at the Midland Hotel with George Chaplin receiving £236 9s 1d from the gate receipts and a collection.

Back in Division One, Bradford City visited Goodison Park where they met one of the most powerful clubs of the era, Everton. Irvine Boocock had a tortuous afternoon and was constantly beaten by Beare which caused Bob Campbell and Bob Torrance to move out of position to cover. Further up the field William Walker and Louis Bookman had come into the side due to injuries and they failed to effectively combine with Jimmy Speirs which left the Scotsman isolated. City were two goals behind before Speirs finally came into the match and scored. He nearly grabbed a late equaliser but City lost 1-2.

A goalless draw with Sheffield Wednesday on a hard, lumpy and frost bound Valley Parade pitch was followed by a heavy defeat at Ewood Park on 7 December. Bradford City conceded five and had it not been for Bob Torrance the score could easily have been doubled. Dickie Bond was once again the target of the Blackburn supporters and an one occasion he pulled up when a whistle was blown in the crowd. At the time of Derby County's visit to Bradford on 14 December, 1912 Bradford City were facing a sustained slump in form. They had not won at home since October and had only won once in six matches. John Clark, making a rare appearance, gave the Bantams an early lead. However it only lasted five minutes before Derby's famous forward Steve Bloomer was left unmarked in the box and he equalised with an unstoppable shot. City's confidence collapsed and they quickly fell 1-3 behind. Peter Logan gave the Bantams late hope when he made it 2-3 but they lost once again in front of their own supporters. Away from Valley Parade, the collapse at Blackburn aside, they were a different proposition. At Tottenham Hotspur they drew 1-1 but threw away several glorious opportunities to take both points. Oscar Fox scored for City but Dickie Bond twice missed with only the keeper to beat and Harry Walden reportedly missed a glaring chance.

Despite the slump, thirty two thousand packed Valley Parade for the Boxing Day match against Middlesbrough. Bradford City's Irish international Louis Bookman was outstanding in the first half and City were reported to have had four shots in the opening three minutes. On the half hour Bookman crossed and Harry Walden scored with a cross-shot. In the second half it began to rain and thick black clouds gathered overhead such that the game was played in semi-darkness. The rain turned torrential and six minutes from time the referee abandoned the match. The frustration was palpable. Middlesbrough were criticised for taking an extra long break at halftime which had left the City players standing around in the rain for several minutes before the second half got underway. In truth it was surprising that the game was allowed to go on for as long as it did with spectators barely being able to follow the play by the time the referee called the game off. Bradford City badly needed the victory and they were now five places off the bottom of the table, albeit with three games in hand.

The despondency among the supporters was not helped when their talisman Jimmy Speirs was sold to second division Leeds City. The decision was prompted by the threat of financial losses and the only way the club could continue to compete in the top division was by selling players when the right offer came along. Though City were a relatively well supported side they could not hope to compete with

"COPE'S" "CLIPS" CIGARETTES

No. 156—SPIERS
Bradford City
Noted Footballers

Jimmy Speirs. Note the incorrect spelling of his surname

the huge attendances and financial resources of the likes of Newcastle United and Aston Villa. Therefore they had little option but to cash in on players with the resulting gamble that it would not undermine their on the field status. Leeds City, then only a second division side with a modest support could rely on heavy financial backing from their local business community given that they were the only professional football team in that city. Already there was evidence of the folly of having two professional clubs competing in a national game in a city the size of Bradford. Thanks to their early success Bradford City had become the club that the wider region supported. The rise of Bradford (PA) and later Huddersfield Town, allied to City's faltering form, was to fatally undermine that status.

Twenty four thousand people witnessed the visit of the league leaders Aston Villa to Valley Parade on 28 December. It was reported that 'brilliant work' by Oscar Fox put City ahead but Villa equalised when a shot that Jock Ewart was certain to save, deflected off Bob Torrance into the net. City came 'within a hairsbreadth' of winning the game when Frank Thompson shot inches wide when through on goal.

The new year opened with two away games in the north west: a single goal defeat at relegation haunted Manchester United on New Year's Day and a narrow 1-2 defeat at Liverpool three days later. In the latter game Oscar Fox gave the Bantams an early lead and it could have been doubled when Frank O'Rourke was pushed in the back in the penalty area. However the referee waved play on, believing that Alex Biggar (making his one and only appearance for City) had a scoring opportunity. Liverpool fought back to defeat City by a single goal.

The FA Cup brought little respite from the gloom that had descended on Valley Parade. Bradford City were drawn away at Newcastle United in the first round on 16 January, 1913 which was possibly the toughest match they could have faced given the Magpie's renowned cup exploits. The match 'aroused extraordinary interest' and excursion trains were even run from Scotland to witness a replay of the 1911 final. The North Eastern Railway Company ran one lengthy train that left Forster Square at five to eight in the morning. Seven of City's cup winning side were in the team that ran out at St James' Park. They were met by 'wild whirling winds and snow and rain'. The weather ruined any hopes of a bumper attendance. Three sides of the ground were open to the elements and the majority of the crowd packed into the covered accommodation.

Jock Ewart

Frank O'Rourke kicked off into the teeth of the gale but after only five minutes Jock Ewart let a cross by George Wilson slip between his hands and into the net. He later claimed to have been blinded by the driving snow. City were constantly defending. The difficulties they faced were illustrated when Ewart cleared the ball up field only to see it blow straight back at him. The Bantams had chances of their own when Frank Thompson shot wide when he seemed a certain scorer. The snow worsened and the match went on in a strange half-light. At half time the referee had no option but to abandon the match to a mixture of relief and disappointment of the fifteen thousand nine hundred crowd.

Across the country eight matches were postponed and another eight abandoned. Bradford (PA) against Barrow was one victim as Bradford was hit by five foot drifts of snow. The City team remained at the Tynemouth base for the scheduled Wednesday replay. However, the weather was unrelenting and the match was put back by a further twenty-four hours. The players returned once again to their now familiar Grand Hotel base but did not get much sleep as a Russian barque ran aground in the stormy seas and was wrecked on the rocks beneath their hotel at Tynemouth! Jock Ewart managed to then cut a finger slicing bread and Mark Mellors was summoned from Bradford as a precaution. The St James' Park pitch was still a quagmire and was liberally coated with sand. The play was farcical and a couple of episodes in particular were reported. Apparently Frank O'Rourke intercepted a pass that had slowed in the mud but when he kicked forward the ball stopped dead and he overran it. The crowd was also in fits of laughter when the referee received a face full of mud and the game had to be stopped whilst he cleared his eyes.

Joe Hargreaves

Bradford City adapted well to the conditions and only great work from Lawrence in the Magpie's goal prevented City from scoring on a couple of occasions. However it was the home side that took the lead when Wilson's high cross-shot passed just underneath the bar on twenty seven minutes. Banks of fog then rolled in from the sea that made it impossible to see from one side of the ground to the other although thankfully these lifted as quickly as they had appeared. In the second half there was 'maximum vigour and minimum football'. Mud and water was by now ankle deep but the referee was determined to complete the match. Semi-darkness then enveloped what was described in the *Bradford Daily Argus* as 'one of the most remarkable cup-ties ever played'. A free kick from Frank Thompson was punched off the line by the Newcastle defender McCracken but it was completely missed in the gloom by the officials. The closing stages of the game were described as 'an absolute farce' but it was played to an unsatisfactory conclusion and City were out of the cup at the first hurdle. Back in Bradford it was reported that City were two goals ahead at half time and all the local papers published that score. It was corrected in later editions but apparently confusion over the result lasted all evening in the city.

The league match against Bolton Wanderers at Valley Parade two days after the cup exit could have been an occasion where the players, fatigued by their long stay in the north east and their exertions on the heavy St James' Park pitch, could have felt sorry for themselves. However, within four minutes City led by two goals. Oscar Fox headed City into a third minute lead and almost straight from the kick off Peter Logan won the ball, beat two men, and scored City's second with a low shot. Fox then hit the crossbar and, after a bone jarring collision between Frank O'Rourke and the Bolton goalkeeper left both laid out on the pitch, Logan tapped City's third goal into the empty net. In the second half City full back Bob Campbell, who had been cautioned in the first

Oscar Fox

period, took revenge on an opponent who had laid out Joe Hargreaves by kicking him wildly. Campbell was sent off for his reaction. Bolton scored, but any faint hopes of a dramatic fight back were extinguished when Archie Devine scored City's fourth. Campbell was suspended for two weeks but at least City had finally won at home at the sixth attempt.

The early exit from the cup caused popular attention to switch across town to Park Avenue. A sixteen thousand crowd - twice the size of that which saw City's victory over Bolton - witnessed Bradford defeat Wolverhampton Wanderers. The discrepancy in the attendances is partly explained by the allure of the FA Cup.

The Bantams' league form continued to be a cause for concern. Despite taking an early lead in their rearranged match with Middlesbrough on 4 February, a bad misjudgement by Jock Ewart allowed the visitors to equalise from long range and Bradford City eventually slumped to another home defeat. However, the crowds were back for the visit of Newcastle United when twenty-two thousand and eight hundred packed into Valley Parade to witness one of the great rivalries of the period. City turned the form book on its head and Frank O'Rourke headed in a Dickie Bond cross at the Bradford End two minutes before the break. The burly Scotsman added a second as the Magpies were outplayed and City won 2-0. The following Saturday Bradford City gained a creditable draw at Oldham Athletic, with Dickie Bond almost winning the match but his shot came back out after hitting the underside of the bar. The Bantams were missing Frank Thompson and Harry Hampton who were both playing for Ireland against England. For the record Thompson was man-of-the-match during Ireland's first ever victory over England and he was carried shoulder high from the pitch by jubilant Irish spectators.

With Bradford (PA) at home to Sheffield Wednesday in the FA Cup the attendance at Valley Parade for the visit of Chelsea on 22 February was nearly eight thousand down on that which witnessed the victory over Newcastle United. Fifteen thousand were at Valley Parade whilst twenty one thousand witnessed the cup tie at Park Avenue and a further five thousand saw Bradford Northern RLFC meet Keighley at Birch Lane – in total forty one thousand people watching professional sport in Bradford at three different venues on a single day. At Valley Parade Chelsea took an early lead after Bob Torrance handled the ball and former City striker Bob Whittingham scored from the penalty spot. Frank Thompson and William Chesser were on the score sheet for City in an entertaining 2-2 draw. There was even an outbreak of local solidarity when news spread that Bradford (PA) had taken the lead in their cup tie and there was reportedly a sporadic round of applause.

Bradford City drew with another London club when Peter Logan scored in a 1-1 stalemate at Woolwich Arsenal. The home crowd threw stones and missiles at Harry Hampton and a bell narrowly missed Jock Ewart in the City goal. The Bradford newspaper writers were unanimous in looking forward to Arsenal's impending move to North London and their new ground at Highbury with the hope that it would improve the behaviour of the crowd.

Whilst Bradford (PA) continued their FA Cup odyssey the following weekend, City had the day off. Aston Villa visited Park Avenue for the FA Cup quarter final and the plum tie attracted twenty five thousand. Although Bradford lost, the cup run had significantly raised the club's profile in Bradford and the surrounding area. The Park Avenue club were now viewed as serious rivals to Bradford City and had overtaken Leeds City as the region's second club.

The Bantams' league slump looked set to continue when they were a goal down to Manchester

C. STORER

BRADFORD CITY

CENTRE HALF

Charlie Storer

City at Valley Parade on 15 March with fifteen minutes remaining. However, a sudden blast of skill and pace from Oscar Fox and Peter Logan saw both men score to give City a narrow lead. In a tense finish Frank O'Rourke headed inches wide and Manchester City broke to put the home goal under siege. However, the Bantams clung on to register a morale boosting victory. In midweek Bob Torrance finally gained long overdue international recognition when he played for the 'Anglo-Scots' against the 'Home-Scots' at Cathkin Park in Glasgow. Also in the 'Anglo-Scots' team was the former City player, and FA Cup winner, David Taylor.

Over a hectic Easter City defeated Notts County with an early Frank O'Rourke goal. Oscar Fox scored in the next four games: a draw at FA Cup semi-finalists West Bromwich Albion, another 1-1 draw at Notts County, a 1-0 victory over Manchester United and finally during the 4-1 thrashing of Everton. In the latter match on 29 March Charlie Storer scored his first ever goal for the club and suddenly City were unbeaten in ten games. However, the run was ended in ignominious fashion at Hillsborough in what the *Bradford Daily Argus* described as 'the Sheffield Slaughter' where Bradford City were thrashed by six goals.

Defeats at home to Blackburn Rovers and at Derby County followed. The visit to Derby was the club's annual trip but as the FA Cup final between Aston Villa and Sunderland was taking place the same day there were not enough available railway carriages to make the venture a success. As a consequence only a fraction of the usual numbers travelled with the Bantams. Dickie Bond was seriously injured at Derby when he collided with an opponent whilst running at full speed. He reportedly fell heavily on the hard ground, dislocated his elbow and had to be taken to hospital in an ambulance. Bradford City's ten men lost 0-4 which meant that in three games they had conceded twelve goals and had not scored themselves.

The final home game of the season brought Tottenham Hotspur to Valley Parade on 26 April, 1913. Making a rare appearance, forward William Walker shot against the post but Charlie Storer was on hand to score from the rebound. Harry Walden then headed a Louis Bookman cross into the net to give City a two goal half-time lead. Walden added a third in the second half and City ended 3-1 victors. After the match, John Nunn (the man largely responsible for overseeing the transformation of Valley Parade into a ground fit for the first division) was presented with a large portrait of the ground and another with the Spion Kop (formerly known as Nunn's Kop) shown full of spectators. The Bantams ended the season with a 0-1 defeat at the League Champions Sunderland on 30 April, 1913.

It was a disappointing campaign and the early exit from the FA Cup had caused a fall in receipts. However record transfer receipts, thanks mainly to the transfer of Jimmy Speirs and Evelyn Lintott - both to second division Leeds City - had brought in £4,115. Players' wages totalled £5,832 – up £300 due to an expanded squad as the reserves now played in the Central League – and incoming transfers had cost £1,280. Therefore City made a profit of £1,210. The bank overdraft, which had been £9,674 in 1911, was now £3,224. Season ticket sales had remained fairly constant and further reduction of the overdraft therefore depended upon success in the FA Cup which is clearly demonstrated by the gate receipts. For example in the 1910/11 FA Cup winning campaign they had been £13,069; in 1911/12, when the club reached the quarter-final: £10,400; and 1912/13, with exit in the first round: £7,180.

The stark fact was that had Bradford City relied on gate receipts alone they would have made a loss in 1912/13. Though the lower gate receipts was almost entirely a result of going out of the FA Cup at the first hurdle, the balance between selling saleable assets and retaining a competitive team was challenging to achieve. As Herbert Hey, owner of the Lumb Lane brewery noted, the club 'needed more share capital' otherwise they would have to continue to run the club on borrowed money. As City were busy balancing the books, across at Park Avenue the deep pockets of the Bradford chairman Harry Briggs allowed them to build a team that was destined to gain first division status. Although there is a danger of labouring the point, the folly of rejecting the 1907 proposal to merge the two Bradford clubs must have been becoming evident to at least some Bradfordians. If the city could bankroll two top class teams one can only wonder what combined resources would have achieved? It is possibly the most frustrating aspect of Bradford's sporting history, namely the inability to see beyond petty localised rivalries. Although those rivalries were very real, in a city the size of Bradford they were simply incompatible with success in a national sport. Had the two clubs combined resources then surely the wealth of Edwardian Bradford would have established a powerful club in the first division and arguably reinforced Bradford's place as the regional centre of the game - a status that was lost irretrievably in the interwar period.

BRADFORD CITY F.C. 1913-14

T.A.EVANS.

CHAPTER SIX

Avenue's Rise, City's Dilemma

1913/14

The 1913/14 season commenced with a sequence of three consecutive drawn matches. During the opening day match against perennial title favourites Aston Villa at Valley Parade, Bradford City were said to be 'always attacking never scoring'. The defence was considered to be particularly strong and when Sheffield United were beaten 2-1 Harry Walden was outstanding. The *Bradford Daily Argus* commented 'the barrackers ceased … Walden enjoyed unstinting support and encouragement. The result was immediately revealed in his excellent display.' In searing heat at Derby the good start to the season seemed set to continue. Though Dickie Bond missed a second minute penalty, Walden was on hand to shoot City ahead a few minutes later. However, in the space of eight minutes the game was turned on its head. Mark Mellors was dazzled by the sun when the home side equalised, a second was added from a free kick and a third from a penalty. A one goal lead had been turned into a 1-3 defeat in a matter of minutes. The extreme heat badly affected the second half and City's George Gane was reduced to walking pace during the last half hour.

The West Riding Cup brought Bradford (PA) to Valley Parade for a midweek fixture. A game of poor finishing exploded into life eight minutes from time. Dickie Bond's cross beat Drabble in the Bradford goal; in a 'frantic rush' for the loose ball, Charlie Storer got there first and scored despite colliding heavily with the post. Bond nearly wrapped the match up but he headed against a post. In the final minute Bradford's Smith beat Bob Campbell to a header and raced away towards the Bradford City goal. He shot past Mark Mellors to give Park Avenue a dramatic late equaliser. The midweek exertions were said to be partly to blame when City conceded a fourth minute goal in their first division match against Manchester City. However, Peter Logan equalised inside eight minutes and before the break the Bantams were 2-1 ahead when the visitors' keeper pushed a Dickie Bond corner into his own net. Thomas Murray later

BRADFORD CITY.   WEDNESDAY, OCT. 8th.

Park Avenue Journal.

OFFICIAL PROGRAMME.   No. 4.   PRICE ONE PENNY.
Edited by "BONG TONG"

This Space Reserved for ———

Helliwell's

1, GODWIN STREET, BRADFORD.

(From 38 and 40 Thornton Road).
Look out for Advertisement on October 11th.

Programme from City's five goal demolition of their neighbours at Park Avenue.

scored a third. Manchester City fought back and set up a tense finish but the Bantams won 3-2. The West Riding Cup replay against Bradford (PA) caused both clubs to state that they would like to be 'excused' from the competition in coming years. However, the County FA had the power to compel the Football League clubs to enter its competition. City were particularly unhappy as they had lost Bob Campbell to injury and Harry Walden with a heavy cold as a result of the West Riding Cup tie. A dismal day and persistent rain reduced the attendance for the replay at Park Avenue. Bradford City seemed determined to finish the contest as quickly as possible. In the third minute Charlie Storer, apparently looking suspiciously offside, crossed for Louis Bookman to score. On eight minutes the roles were reversed when Bookman crossed for Storer to head in City's second. Two minutes later Peter Logan hit a third after a Dickie Bond freekick was parried. In the seventeenth minute City were awarded a penalty when Dainty handled the ball whilst protecting his face from a fierce shot. The Bradford keeper Mason blocked Oscar Fox's free kick with his legs but Fox was on hand to tap in the rebound and Bradford City were 4-0 ahead. In the second period City completed the scoring with a spectacular fifth. Bond broke at pace and Storer headed Bond's cross to Bookman who played an immediate cross back in from the opposite wing for Storer to place the ball past a stranded Smith.

Louis Bookman was absent from City's trip to Tottenham Hotspur on 11 October 1913 due to a Jewish religious festival. Though the attack was slightly blunted, the defence was its usual miserly self and Irvine Boocock excelled as he dealt with the threat of Spurs' winger Walden who the *Bradford Daily Argus* described as 'the Tottenham midget who is as elusive as an eel'. The goalless draw was followed by a trip to Ewood Park to face the Division One leaders Blackburn Rovers who had won seven and drawn one of their opening matches. They had a 'Bank of England forward line' which had cost an incredible six thousand pounds. To put that figure in context, the average wage for a skilled man was around £80 a year. City's train arrived in Blackburn ninety minutes late. The team apparently got into a single motor car which then immediately suffered a puncture. It kept going but it was reportedly an extremely bumpy ride for the players. Dickie Bond, ever the individual, commandeered a horse drawn cab and arrived serenely at the ground seconds behind the packed car. A quick change in the dressing room and the players were hurried onto the

Irvine Boocock

pitch and the kick off was delayed by only seven minutes. With Liverpool and Middlesbrough both conceding seven at Ewood Park many feared the worst, especially in light of the chaotic arrival. However, the players had other ideas. From the off they harried their illustrious opponents and gave them no time to settle on the ball. Bob Torrance, 'with his usual terrier-like tenacity', fairly smothered Rovers' free scoring forward Clennel. However, it was the emerging talent of Irvine Boocock who took the eye. The 'Spen Valley youngster' was the best player on the field and was at the heart of City's fine defensive effort. Indeed, had Bond shown a bit more composure the Bantams could have recorded a remarkable victory.

The tough games kept coming. Next on 25 October 1913, it was the champions Sunderland at Valley Parade. Unfortunately, after only ten minutes Jimmy McDonald limped off. He had wrenched a muscle and would be out of action for several months. The thirty thousand crowd was enthralled by City's gutsy defensive display. For nearly an hour the ten men held firm until Bob Campbell was caught out by the Sunderland winger Richardson The burly full back lunged in and the referee awarded a penalty despite Campbell's insistence that he had played the ball and that the winger had 'fallen over him'. The resistance was broken; the champions scored again and City were beaten for only the second time in the season. Louis Bookman scored in a creditable 1-1 draw at Everton the following Saturday and the Bantams' season was back on track. This was followed by a 1-0 victory at home to West Bromwich Albion that was put down to Bradford City's good use of their 'flying wingers' Bond and Bookman on the heavy pitch.

Bond was in fine form when Bradford City visited Sheffield Wednesday on 15 November 1913. Though the Owls went one up following confusion between George Robinson and Jimmy McIlvenny, Bond soon had the Bantams back in the ascendancy. McIlvenny made amends for his earlier error by equalising with a header from a Bond cross. He then headed another against the post before Charlie Storer headed two more to give City a 3-1 victory. Bolton Wanderers, third in the table, were next to face City's flying wingers on 22 November. After only ten minutes Fox and Storer combined and the former scored with a shot that the visiting keeper could not hold. A few minutes later Bond crossed and Storer's header was parried, from which the wily Fox shot City into a two goal lead. A third beckoned when Wanderers' keeper Edmondson dropped the ball right on the goal line. Storer, who could have tapped the ball in, shot wide 'in miraculous fashion'. Bolton reduced the arrears shortly before the half-time break but any fears among the home fans were soon extinguished when Oscar Fox hit a second half hat-trick. City won 5-1 and Fox had scored four. 'Bolton Bamboozled' was the *Bradford Daily Argus* headline. Bradford City were up to sixth in the table and many were beginning to eye the summit itself. Nine goals in three straight wins had the City fans dreaming of silverware.

The City team that 'bamboozled' Bolton

The difficult trip to big spending Chelsea on 29 November became all but impossible when Bob Campbell pulled a thigh muscle and had to retire after half an hour. City were already one goal behind and now faced an hour with only ten men. However, when Oscar Fox scored his sixth goal in four games the depleted Bantams were level. With another tremendous rearguard action City held off Chelsea until three minutes from time when Vivian Woodward's header from a free kick finally broke their brave resistance. It was only Bradford City's third defeat of the season. The injury to Campbell brought the inexperienced Fred Potts into the side for the visit of Oldham Athletic to Valley Parade on 6 December. It was Bob Torrance's benefit game and twenty thousand cheered as Torrance led City out. The brass band played 'Scottish airs'. It was a disappointing match with the defences on top. A couple of minutes from time the visitors stole the points when the Oldham forward Gee kicked Jock Ewart's hand as the City goalkeeper was about to pick up the ball. The Scottish international lost the ball and Gee was free to score into an open net. At least Torrance's benefit gained the renowned defender £520. As City were losing to Oldham, Bradford (PA) were going top of the second division.

Two consecutive defeats were followed by three consecutive draws. At Manchester United, on 13 December, Billy Meredith's 'bewildering footwork' led to United's Knowles scoring a sensational goal from forty yards. Straight from the restart Storer and McIlvenny exchanged passes at pace through the home defence and Storer shot Bradford City level. In the week leading up to the home game against Burnley on 20 December it was reported that a tango dance craze was sweeping

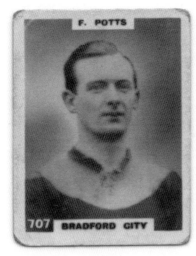

F. POTTS

707 BRADFORD CITY

Fred Potts

Bradford. There was a special cheer from the Valley Parade crowd for returning FA Cup winner David Taylor in the visitors' ranks. The footwork of Burnley's famous international forward Freeman gave the visitors an early lead, partly due to a misunderstanding between Bob Torrance and Fred Potts. The brilliance of Jerry Dawson in the Burnley goal kept City at bay until Jimmy McIlvenny equalised. The third draw in the sequence came in a goalless stalemate against Newcastle United at St James' Park on Christmas Day.

The Magpies travelled to Bradford the following day and a crowd of thirty two thousand jammed into Valley Parade for the Boxing Day encounter between the two old adversaries. Oscar Fox opened the scoring following a weak clearance in the sixth minute. Ten minutes later City were two ahead when Charlie Storer neatly controlled debutant John Brennan's lob, beat his marker Hudspeth and scored with a shot high into the net. Storer hit a post in the second half as Bradford City outplayed their illustrious visitors. The third game in as many days came at Villa Park where a moment of brilliance from Dickie Bond gave City a famous victory.

New Year's Day 1914 took the Bantams to Anfield where once again Bond was the difference between the sides. Eight minutes from time, neat passing between Storer, Logan and Bond saw the latter score from close range to give City a 1-0 victory. Three victories and a draw in four games in seven days had taken City's young side to fifth place in the table. Fred Potts, Joe Hargreaves, Irvine Boocock and Charlie Storer had established themselves in a side that was beginning to emerge as serious contenders for the Football League championship. They were the new faces who had replaced the likes of Jimmy Speirs, David Taylor and Evelyn Lintott.

However, the visit of Middlesbrough to Valley Parade, (accompanied by three thousand visiting supporters conveyed on five special trains enjoying their club's annual trip), was described as the 'muddle in the mud'. Inside fifteen minutes Bradford City were two goals behind. The frustration of the home crowd threatened to boil over and the referee was forced to halt the game and caution a spectator for making 'an improper remark'. Jimmy McIlvenny reduced the arrears with an 'unstoppable drive' before half time. Unfortunately, a heavy back pass by Irvine Boocock early in the second period beat Jock Ewart, and despite a frantic scramble, Boro's Tinsley placed the ball into the empty net and City were 1-3 behind. Peter Logan hit the post and Charlie Storer headed in a Dickie Bond cross to make it 2-3. Despite intense pressure in the final ten minutes Boro held on and City lost by the odd goal in five.

The FA Cup draw was kind to City bringing Arsenal to Valley Parade – a game the Bantams were expected to win at a canter. In preparation the City players walked on Ilkley and Baildon moors 'in search of health giving breezes'. They then spent their evenings together at the Midland Hotel. Bradford (Park Avenue) had also been drawn at home in the FA Cup to Reading. The morning of the FA Cup games saw six hundred Reading supporters arrive in the city centre, some of whom wore biscuits hung from their lapels (which was a reference to the club's nickname). They were apparently confused by the name Tyrrel Street which they had been given as the place to catch trams to Park Avenue. A smaller group of Arsenal supporters arrived shortly after but without much show and they melted away into the city crowds. Dismal weather and heavy rain had made the Valley Parade pitch very heavy. Twenty thousand saw Dickie Bond score a brace to ease City into the second round. When Bond scored his first he 'jumped a yard into the air' in celebration. His second was a Bond classic: he beat his marker, drew the Arsenal keeper and scored with a well placed shot. In between Bond's goals Charlie Storer also struck a post.

Back in the Division One Bradford City drew 1-1 at Sheffield United on 17 January 1914. This was a creditable point given that they were missing Campbell, Robinson and Fox. Another

Bradford City's 1913/14 team

stalemate followed when City and Derby County fought out a goalless draw. Again City were depleted by injuries with George Wild making his debut in for the absent Jimmy McIlvenny. Apparently, the biggest cheer of the game came when two famous internationals, the Bantams' Dickie Bond and the Rams' Steve Bloomer, met in the centre circle for the toss up.

The second round of the FA Cup took the Bantams to Millwall of Division Two. Oscar Fox suffered a serious gash to his wrist whilst pouring a jug of water at the team's hotel. Though he played he was completely off form. Millwall's Davies beat Jock Ewart by inches to give the home side a shock lead. Although City had a big appeal for a penalty turned down late in the match, they were convincingly beaten by the Lions. It was a desperately disappointing exit from the FA Cup as much was expected from the emerging side.

The goalkeepers were the centre of attention when Bradford City visited Manchester City at Hyde Road on 7 February 1914. Frank O'Rourke, making his first appearance of the season, charged the home goalkeeper and both the custodian and the ball ended up in the back of the net. In an age when the charging of keeper in possession of the ball was allowed O'Rourke thought he had scored. However, the referee disallowed it claiming that the goalkeeper had been shoulder charged before he had caught the ball. At the other end Jock Ewart decided to leave a long ball as he thought it was going out for a corner. However, he changed his mind and ran towards the slow moving ball. He was beaten to it, the ball was crossed and a home striker had the simple task of tapping it into the empty net. The Scotsman's error cost City the game as they lost 0-1. Tottenham Hotspur were beaten 2-1 by goals from Storer and Fox but the outside chances of the league title disappeared when City lost 0-2 at leaders Blackburn Rovers.

It was frustrating, for when Bradford City won at Roker Park (their first ever victory over Sunderland on their home ground) they had taken fifteen points from fourteen away games when a victory was worth two points. City were in fourth place but were nine points adrift of Blackburn Rovers. The economic might of the leaders was illustrated when they signed forward Percy Dawson for two thousand pounds This brought Blackburn's spending on forwards alone to eight thousand pounds for the season which was eight hundred pounds more than City's gate receipts for the entire 1912/13 season. Though City were building a side which looked likely to challenge for honours in the

George Robinson

near future, they were facing sides with either much larger attendances – such as Newcastle United and Aston Villa – or clubs like Blackburn Rovers who had wealthy backers. The Bantams' manager, Peter O'Rourke, was doing a tremendous job but brutal economics were stacked against him.

George 'Geordie' Robinson enjoyed a well-earned benefit match at home to Everton on 7 March 1914. The gate receipts, combined with a collection including a half a guinea from Jimmy Speirs, came to five hundred pounds. Whatever the politics surrounding benefit matches there can be no doubt that Robinson was a worthy recipient. He had played in City's first ever match in September 1903, captained the second division championship winning side of 1908 and appeared in the 1911 FA Cup Final. Unfortunately, the visitors won the match with an eighteenth minute goal. Another single goal defeat at West Bromwich Albion was followed by a morale boosting 3-1 victory over relegation threatened Sheffield Wednesday at Valley Parade. Missing from the Yorkshire derby was Irvine Boocock whose rapid progression was recognised by selection for the English League v Scottish League representative match played at Turf Moor, Burnley.

The season began to drift away from the Bantams. A three goal defeat at Bolton on 28 March was only kept respectable by the brilliant form of Jock Ewart – although City did twice hit the post. Only ten thousand witnessed the visit of Chelsea to Bradford. The scoreless draw attracted the headline 'Paraders in a Pickle'. The match was said to be 'a sad disappointment'. A 1-2 defeat at bottom club Preston North End combined with a 1-3 loss at Oldham left everyone connected with the club looking forward to the summer break. Though an experimental line up clinched a 1-0 victory over Liverpool, with Irvine Boocock scoring the only goal of his entire City career, the season could not end soon enough. A 1-1 draw at home to Manchester United and a 2-2 draw at Burnley completed the campaign.

City's visit to Turf Moor was the home side's first game since they had won the FA Cup. A celebratory forty thousand crowd gathered to cheer their heroes. However, Bradford City, and particularly Dickie Bond, spoiled the party. Bond scored twice and the Bantams were two up at the break. A penalty by former City player David Taylor made it 1-2 and then two minutes from time the referee awarded Burnley a controversial equaliser. The ball was cleared off the Bradford City line but the crowd roared and the referee awarded a goal despite protestations that the ball had been at least two inches away from the line when it was cleared.

Though City ended in a creditable ninth there was great disappointment that the excellent defence and early form, particularly away from home, had not been built on. A *Bradford Daily Argus* headline summing up the season said 'Scarcity of Goals: defence strong, better forwards wanted'.

As City were involved in the dramatic final game at Turf Moor, Bradford (Park Avenue) were clinching promotion to Division One. City manager Peter O'Rourke telephoned his congratulations to their neighbours' celebration dinner at the Midland Hotel. Bradford now had two first division football clubs which was quite a feat, albeit one largely bank-rolled by Harry Briggs, the owner of Bradford (PA). Fred Lintott, the brother of former City midfielder Evelyn Lintott, was City's reporter for the *Bradford Daily Argus*. The newspaper was the voice of Bradford's Tories, so perhaps it was no surprise that he stated that he was 'an out and out opponent of amalgamation … and that what

Bradford wanted was two first division clubs with competitive rivalry as an ever present stimulus'. This free market ethos was a corner stone of the business and economic thinking of the time but events were to prove that it could not be applied to a national sporting competition. Bradford simply did not have the population or economic backing to sustain two first division football clubs. The summer of 1914 marked a high point for Bradford football and arguably the economic confidence of the city. It was an illusion. The Great War would accelerate changes to world economics that would undermine the city's industrial base. That in turn would have a profound impact on Bradford's two professional clubs.

Bradford City's dilemma was summed up at their annual meeting at the Mechanics' Institute in the city centre on 12 June. The club fully recognised that they needed a more powerful forward line to supplement their renowned defence. However, heavy transfer fees had to be weighed against reducing the club's debt. Over the preceding eleven years twenty thousand pounds had been spent on building the team whereas fifteen thousand pounds had been raised by the sale of players. The overdraft at the bank was now down to £2,310. The club was caught on the horns of a dilemma and one that had become all the more urgent with the promotion of Bradford (Park Avenue) to Division One. Should they invest in a new forward line and hope that it would bring success in the FA Cup and the first division, or continue their policy of balancing building the team, whilst steadily reducing the overdraft? The early exits from the FA Cup had cost the club dearly over the previous two seasons. Now they had the added danger of Bradford (PA) being poised to entice away floating supporters if City faltered. The formation of Leeds City and Huddersfield Town had partly eroded the Bantams regional support and now they faced competition within their own city. Only further success on the field would cement City's position as the region's dominant club.

Peter O'Rourke

The great rivals of the Edwardian era, Bradford City and Newcastle United, in action at Valley Parade.

CHAPTER SEVEN

The Bantams in Europe

One hundred years ago there was such prestige associated with winning the FA Cup that the winners were invited to play in Europe in exhibition games. A European tour was nothing new for the Bantams as they had toured Belgium and Germany in the summer of 1908. However they broke new ground following their FA Cup triumph when they visited Scandinavia. The cup winners based themselves in the Danish capital of Copenhagen and one of their matches was watched by Prince Aage, a son of the King of Denmark. The tour ended with a match in Sweden against a national eleven which the Swedes won by a single goal. It was the first time an English club had ever lost to a Swedish side and it reportedly prompted huge celebrations.

The summer of 1914 saw City back in Europe, this time on a comprehensive ten game tour of Germany and Switzerland. The Bantams won nine of those fixtures including heavy victories at the future footballing centres of Stuttgart and Munich. The only defeat came at Frankfurt. The circumstances of the defeat were strange to say the least. It was reported that throughout the match a zeppelin flew over the ground. It was the first time any of the players had seen such a sight and apparently they spent the majority of the game watching the giant airship. Accordingly the 1-3 defeat was attributed to the distraction!

The tour took place just three months before the Great War broke out. After a tough game at Stuttgart, Jock Ewart (who was to suffer badly from shell shock during the war) is reported to have said that 'if the Germans fight like they play football, we are in for a rough time'.

Cup Winners on Board the s.s. Salmo, Outward Bound, in Hull Docks.
Reading from left to right:—Mr. C. E. Craven ("Observer"), Mr. Peter O'Rourke,
Jock Young, David Taylor, Frank Thompson, Martin Spendiff, Frank O'Rourke, James
Speirs, James Blair, Geo. Robinson, Dickie Bond, James McIlvenny, Willie Gildea
and Bob Torrance.

CHAPTER EIGHT

The Beginning of the Fall

1914/15

Not surprisingly the outbreak of the Great War utterly dominated Bradford's newspapers and virtually every page was given over to reporting of the war. The expectation was that the war would reduce interest in sport. However, the pre-season practice matches of both Bradford clubs attracted higher than usual crowds. The exceptionally fine weather, allied to a communal spirit, was said to be responsible for the large pre-season attendances. Therefore whilst British soldiers fought and died at Le Cateau, thousands of their fellow countrymen enjoyed the carefree atmosphere of the practice matches. However the takings from City's practice matches, £106 4s 4d, were donated to the War Relief Fund and the Bradford Hospital Fund.

A week before the start of the campaign City's season ticket sales were one hundred pounds higher than the previous season. The rise was partially explained by the fact that many had decided not to take a holiday and had spent part of their holiday money on season tickets. A restriction on rail travel had undoubtedly affected the holiday trade but the pattern of spending probably reflected with widespread belief that the war would be short-lived. In the event the usual late surge of season ticket sales did not materialise and overall sales were down £715 on the 1913/14 season.

The 1914/15 season opened with a catastrophic 1-4 defeat at Manchester City. A reconstructed team failed to play as a unit and Frank Buckley, one of City's expensive summer signings, played too close to the forward line leaving the defence exposed. The Bantams were three goals down at half-time. The manager Peter O'Rourke rectified some of the failings during the interval and Albert Shepherd, another new signing, scored for City. There was a vast improvement at Burnley during the second match of the campaign. The kick off was put back to 5.30pm due to a cricket match taking place on the Turf Moor ground. The attendance was only ten thousand, a quarter of that which had witnessed the draw between the two sides just over four months previously. Oscar Fox scored the only goal of the game after eighteen minutes. The *Bradford Daily Argus* commented that although the victory over the FA Cup holders was enjoyed by the travelling City supporters, 'a win and a loss on the football field is but a minor episode in these stirring times'.

The opening home match of the season, a 2-2 draw with Chelsea, saw a sprinkling of khaki uniforms among the fourteen thousand crowd – the soldiers had been admitted free of charge. Despite the significant donations made by both Bradford clubs to the War Relief Fund, the free admission of soldiers and the acknowledgement that football offered valuable relief from the worries of wartime, unflattering comparisons were made with the response of the local rugby union clubs. Heaton had provided thirty players to the armed forces and Baildon ten. It was arguably unfair as the rugby union players were amateurs and, given their backgrounds, would have been more likely to have been army reservists. Indeed, the links between the rugby union game and the army were close as rugby union had long been the game of choice for the establishment. In contrast, professional footballers were generally working class men with little social opportunity, or peer pressure, to have been army reservists. With the popular belief that the war would be 'over by Christmas' why would a professional footballer interrupt his career, and risk injury, if it was all to be completed in twelve weeks?

Though the continuation of football attracted adverse comment, pleas to retain the subscription classical music concerts at St George's Hall was supported by some of those who criticised the stance of the Football League. Among the largely working class supporters of football there appears to have been little pressure for the cancellation of the league competition. Sport had continued through the Boer War and such was the belief that the Great War would be 'over by Christmas' the prevailing attitude was that normal life should continue.

Oscar Fox began the season where he had left off with four goals in the first four games. The draw with Chelsea was followed by another Valley Parade stalemate, this time a 2-2 draw against Spurs and then a single goal defeat at Newcastle United. Despite the growing travel restrictions a large contingent of Middlesbrough supporters were among the twenty thousand crowd at Valley Parade to witness a 1-1 draw on 26 September 1914. Bradford City led when Sam Anderson, yet another newly signed forward player, scored. However Harry Walden was carried off with a twisted knee shortly afterwards and Middlesbrough equalised against the ten men. Another 1-1 draw at Sheffield Wednesday followed, this time with Dickie Bond scoring for City.

The war was beginning to impact on attendances and hit the finances of the clubs. A proposal was tabled that players on the maximum wage of £5 a week would forfeit 15% of their income and those on £2 would lose 5%, with the money raised being used to give financial assistance to clubs struggling to pay their players' wages. The League Management Committee revealed that there had been a 50% reduction in attendances across both the first and second division's. At least six second division clubs were in 'grave danger' of financial collapse. The wage reductions, and a partial pooling of gate money, was seen as vital if the integrity of the Football League was to be protected.

The highest crowd of the season thus far to witness any Bradford City game, home or away, was attracted to Valley Parade for the visit of Aston Villa on 10 October. Among the twenty five

thousand crowd were around two thousand soldiers, including the bulk of the newly formed Bradford Pals battalion who were all admitted free of charge. The Pals were based at the Valley Parade barracks almost directly behind the Main Stand, so the links with the club must have been particularly close. Of course, one of those links was the claret and amber colours of the West Yorkshire Regiment, which was the inspiration when City's predecessors adopted the distinct colours in 1884. The Bradford Church Lads' Brigade collected money for the Lord Mayor's War Fund and cigarettes for the soldiers. Oscar Fox rose to the occasion by hitting a second half hat-trick as City won emphatically 3-0.

Despite reduced attendances there was plenty of entertainment on show. Fox struck the crossbar inside the first twenty minutes at Liverpool and Peter Logan hit the post as City's forwards dominated the opening exchanges. Sam Anderson scored for the Bantams and Jock Ewart saved two penalties. However, it was all in vain as Bradford City lost 1-2.

The first ever Football League derby between the Bradford clubs at Valley Parade took place on

Oscar Fox

24 October 1914. It was a thrilling encounter. Charlie Storer, Oscar Fox and Jimmy McIlvenny scored as City defeated Bradford 3-2. However, the game was overshadowed by the war. The 29,802 crowd heard repeated appeals for recruits. At half-time the former president of both Manningham and Bradford City, Alfred Ayrton, made a short, but rousing, speech, which was followed by showers of money and cigarettes. The Football League finally agreed in late October that clubs would deposit 2½% of gate receipts to a common fund that would be used to aid clubs suffering from financial difficulties. The players also agreed to accept wage reductions on a sliding scale depending on their wage level.

A hotly disputed penalty conceded by Irvine Boocock at Oldham on 31 October condemned City to a 0-1 defeat. This was to be the last defeat until Boxing Day. Twenty-three goals in seven games improved City's prospect. Manchester United were the first victims when they visited Valley Parade on 7 November. The first goal was unfortunate for the visitors as United's Hunter accidentally handled when he was pushed in the back by

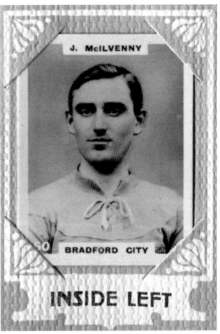

Jimmy McIlvenny

Charlie Storer. The referee awarded a penalty and the prolific Oscar Fox added to his tally from the spot to put City 1-0 ahead. The United players refused to retrieve the ball from the back of the net in protest at the award of the penalty. However, a small boy jumped over the perimeter wall and kicked the ball back into play. The contentious penalty may have been on the referee's mind when he waved away appeals for what was said to be a 'definite penalty' when Peter Logan was brought down inside the box. However, it wasn't long before Storer extended City's lead and the drastically reduced twelve thousand crowd – less than half of the near thirty thousand which had seen the Bradford derby – enjoyed a 4-2 victory for the Bantams. Manchester United escaped an even heavier defeat when Fox contrived to miss a second half penalty.

Across Division One attendances continued to plummet as recruitment took thousands away into the armed services or into long hours of war related work. It was noted that very few visiting supporters were now travelling with their teams. The railways were at full stretch and the excursion carriages, which once carried thousands of football supporters, were now taking soldiers to the Channel ports and the front. A paltry eight thousand saw City's visit to Bolton Wanderers. The City supporters in the crowd were treated to a five-goal salvo, of which Oscar Fox scored four. By all accounts he should have had five but he missed another penalty. Amazingly Bolton had taken an early lead but such was City's dominance that one reporter commented that the 5-3 victory really should have been much greater and City could have scored eight. Oscar Fox was now the first division's leading scorer with thirteen goals in thirteen games.

Fog threatened Blackburn Rovers' visit to Bradford on 21 November. An early kick off was agreed as a combination of fading light and the fog would have undoubtedly caused the match to be abandoned. The early start reduced the attendance to twelve thousand. One of the linesmen could not get to Bradford due to chaos on the railways caused by the thick fog and heavy traffic of men and materials for the war effort. In the absence of a qualified linesman in the ground a coin was tossed to decide which manager would replace the absent official. City's Peter O'Rourke ran the line and by a coincidence the former City player Jimmie Roberts was the referee. The league champions were swept aside as Bradford City won 3-0. The only surprise was that Oscar Fox didn't score. Jimmy McDonald and a brace from Dickie Bond cemented City's top five place in the First Division table.

Bradford ✦ City
A. F. C.

Official Team Card
For CENTRAL LEAGUE GAMES.

Wilkinson and Woodhouse, Printers, Morley Street, Bradford.

No. 6   NOV. 28th, 1914   PRICE ONE PENNY.

Editor's Note Book

By defeating Manchester United, Bolton Wanderers and Blackburn Rovers, the Paraders have established a gain of five League points on last season.

The three matches were won with a total score of 12-5, whereas last season only one point was obtained from the three games, and the total score was 1-6.

Such a conclusive defeat of the Rovers has caused many critics suddenly to discover that there are some fine players in the Bradford City team.

We are told Fox and Bond were in International form last Saturday, but they have played just as well in other games this season.

It was confidently expected that Irvine Boocock would be chosen to play for the North against England in the first Trial match, but the powers that be have indefinitely postponed the fixture.

Oscar Fox kept the lead amongst the goal-scorers, although he failed to notch one last week. Parker, of Everton, got three and that made him 13, or one less than the popular Parader.

Bond would be more than delighted with his two goals against the Rovers. He has not forgotten his many battles at Ewood Park as a Prestonian.

If he scores two at a time he will make the lodger jealous. The right wing pair have bagged 18 out of City's 27. The other nine are spread out in pairs and singles, Anderson, Storer and Shepherd have two each, and McIlvenny, Logan and McDonald one each.

At Blackburn, the City Reserves had an unlucky afternoon.

Anderson gave them the lead in the first half, and the second half was well advanced before the Rovers equalised as the result of a penalty against Brown.

Later on Chaplin was injured and had to retire, and during his absence the Rovers scored two more. Eventually they won 4-1.

During the first half the Paraders had chances enough to have put the result beyond all doubt.

On Wednesday there was a very poor game, and when four minutes

---

RED FLAG   KEY BOARD.   WHITE FLAG

A	BLACKBURN ROV.		A	THE ARSENAL	1
B	BURNLEY		B	BRISTOL CITY	
	NOTTS COUNTY	0		BIRMINGHAM	2
C	BRADFORD CITY		C	BLACKPOOL	
	BOLTON WANDERERS	2		CLAPTON ORIENT	0
D	TOTTENHAM HOTS.	1	D	BURY	
	BRADFORD			FULHAM	1
E	SHEFFIELD UN.	0	E	BARNSLEY	1
	LIVERPOOL	0		WOLVERHAMPTON W.	0
F	ASTON VILLA	5	F	GLOSSOP	0
	MANCHESTER UN.	1		LEEDS CITY	1
G	NEWCASTLE UNITED	0	G	PRESTON N.E.	
	SUNDERLAND			DERBY COUNTY	1
H	CHELSEA	0	H	HUDDERSFIELD T.	1
	SHEFFIELD WED.	0		HULL CITY	
I	EVERTON		I	NOTTS FOREST	0
	OLDHAM ATHLETIC	2		LINCOLN CITY	
J	MIDDLESBROUGH	8	J	GRIMSBY TOWN	4
	WEST BROMWICH			STOCKPORT O.	1
	MANCHESTER CITY	0		LEICESTER FOSSE	

TO FOOTBALL CROWDS.

There are approximately 3,000,000 men with no family responsibility playing in and watching football matches. I ask these to show that they are good sportsmen and to enlist now, and help the other good sportsmen who are so bravely fighting Britain's battle against the world's enemy.—Mr. F. J. Wall, secretary of the Football Association.

Reserve team programme for a game played on 20th November 1914. Note the exhortations to encourage enlistment.

A visit to bottom placed Notts County should have been a simple task for the free scoring Bantams but a goalless draw ensued and City slipped into sixth place in the table. The goals returned when Sunderland were thrashed 3-0. Winger Craig Brown scored on his debut. The 'boisterous weather' meant another early kick off and the resulting six thousand crowd was the then lowest ever crowd at Valley Parade for a Saturday league match. Though the early kick off was a factor it was also noted that ten thousand Bradford men were now in military service. Among those numbers were twenty one Bradford Northern Rugby League Club players. The toll of war was also becoming apparent with photographs of Bradford men who had been killed, wounded or captured appearing on a daily basis in the newspapers.

A thrilling 3-3 draw at Sheffield Wednesday on 12 December saw summer signing Albert Shepherd score twice. The former Newcastle United forward was beginning to find form, scoring four in five games. His partnership with Oscar Fox was shaping up to be a formidable one indeed. City's renowned defence, allied to this new strike force, should have launched the club on a new exciting era. As events later conspired, it was not to be. Shepherd added to his tally scoring a hat-trick as West Bromwich Albion were demolished 5-0 at Valley Parade on 19 December. Sadly, only five thousand three hundred saw the game. The war was frustrating City's well-laid plans. On Christmas Day 1914 Shepherd scored a tremendous goal direct from a free kick to give City a share of the points at Goodison Park. Everton travelled to Valley Parade for the rematch on Boxing Day and it was to be the last of the huge attendances before the war halted the league programme. Thirty five thousand crammed into the ground. Many were in uniform and apparently there was a strange atmosphere. Perhaps it was recognised as the last great gathering before many would leave for the front and never return? City's two great marksmen were affected by the occasion. Shepherd hit a post and Fox the bar. Then Everton scored the only goal of the game and Bradford City lost 0-1. It was the first defeat since October.

Bradford City welcomed 1915 with a home match against the FA Cup holders Burnley. In the first minute a passing move between Bob Torrance, Dickie Bond, Albert Shepherd, and James Marshall saw the latter shoot but Dawson in the Clarets' goal was equal to it. Heavy pressure was placed on the visitors' goal. Albert Shepherd scored but the whistle had already gone. The Burnley goalkeeper is reported to have saved 'brilliantly' from Oscar Fox. Jimmy McDonald had a shot headed off the line. City did everything but score. In the second half Bond retired with a muscle strain and the Bantams were reduced to ten men. Bob Torrance was outstanding as City's depleted ranks played out a goalless draw. The *Bradford Daily Argus* said:

'Torrance was amazing. He raced here there and everywhere at a pace which would have used up two or three ordinary mortals. Peter Pan is described as the boy who refuses to grow up and Torrance may well claim to be the half back who refuses to grow tired!'

The FA Cup first round saw City travel to Northern League side Darlington. The home side shaded the first half but City came into their own after the break and comfortably saw out the game. A 'remarkable' goal by Albert Shepherd separated the sides. A few days after the cup tie twelve

Bob Torrance

73

Jimmy McIlvenny

hundred men of the first Bradford Pals battalion marched out of the Valley Parade skating rink en route to training in the Dales. The majority of them would never return.

Back in the Division One, Bradford City's visit to Tottenham Hotspur on 16 January 1915 turned into possibly the greatest defensive display of the club's entire history. After twenty minutes Jimmy McIlvenny and Albert Shepherd were both sent off. McIlvenny was dismissed after twice fouling the home favourite Freddie Walden, whom the *Bradford Daily Argus* commented acidly 'ought to be kept in a glass case'. The crowd reaction was felt to have influenced the referee. Albert Shepherd questioned the decision and was sent off for dissent. His four word outburst was the subject of vastly differing interpretations after the game. It was the first time either player had been sent off in their careers. The nine men became just eight when Irvine Boocock became the third City player to be dismissed. The depleted ranks included Dickie Bond who was only half-fit. The home crowd, who were initially hostile to the City players, slowly began to appreciate the fighting qualities of the eight men. Indeed, in the final twenty minutes they were actively urging the Bantams to cling on and when the whistle sounded, with the match scoreless, the City players were given a huge ovation.

Newcastle United were the next visitors to Valley Parade. The Magpies took and early lead but Bradford City struck back to equalise. Injuries reduced the visitors to nine men but City could not break through and the match ended in a frustrating 1-1 draw. The single point kept the Bantams in sixth place in the First Division table, a position they had been in since November!

The FA Cup second round brought Middlesbrough to Valley Parade on 30 January 1915. In a high paced match a Dickie Bond goal was enough to take Bradford City into the third round. The attendance of 26,457 was impressive given the background against which it was played and reinforced the huge popularity of the FA Cup. As the cup tie raged, the Bradford Pals battalion football team was playing a friendly match against Gargrave in the Yorkshire Dales. All five goals were scored by Private Rawnsley. City could have benefited from such prowess in front of goal when they visited Middlesbrough for a Division One game four days' after the FA Cup tie. Boro gained revenge beating City 0-3. The Bantams' line up was radically changed from the FA Cup tie. Following their antics at Spurs Jimmy McIlvenny was starting a month's suspension and Albert Shepherd fourteen days. As two of City's forwards sat out the match another, Oscar Fox, was badly injured. It was the Bantams first away defeat since October.

The injuries and suspensions meant that only four regular first team players appeared in the home match with Sheffield United. The 'Blades' were behind on eighteen minutes when Charlie Storer played in Sam Anderson who scored with a straight drive. The visitors equalised in the second half prompting the comment that Bradford City had played out 'their usual draw'. It was harsh given that what was effectively a second eleven had held their own against an established first division side. Given the continuing selection problems a draw at Aston Villa was quite a feat. Jock Ewart had a relatively quiet afternoon in the City goal and the one time he was beaten Jimmy McDonald was there to clear the danger. The press wondered where City would have been in the league table had they not suffered such debilitating injuries since the turn of the year.

The FA Cup third round saw Norwich City return to Valley Parade. The Canaries' visit prompted memories of their trip north in 1911 when City won the FA Cup. Once again a difficult tie was anticipated as Norwich had beaten Nottingham Forest and Tottenham Hotspur in the previous rounds. As the visitors emerged, 'in their canary uniforms' from the tunnel under the Spion Kop, the *Bradford Daily Argus* noted that 'they were a big hefty lot'. Two fabulous saves from Joe Lansdale in the visitors net kept the score line blank. Albert Shepherd eventually broke the deadlock but the match ended in a 1-1 draw. It was doubly frustrating for City as the replay caused the scheduled first division Bradford derby match at Park Avenue to be postponed. The replay at Carrow Road was a culture shock for the visiting press crops. Used to the grand first division grounds one made the sniffy comment 'they call it "the Nest". It would be more appropriate to describe it as a second rate poultry run'. The long journey to Norfolk had been badly disrupted due to the heavy war traffic on the railways. The match, played on a sloping greasy pitch, saw the defences on top and very few scoring chances. Even thirty minutes extra time failed to separate the sides. Apparently, the game was 'more vigour than polish'. A crowd of 8,043 witnessed the draw. Hardly any Bradfordians were in attendance as no railway excursions were organised.

The stalemate left the Football Association in a quandary. They had banned midweek cup ties in order to avoid distracting vital war work. They ordered that the tie be replayed behind closed doors at Lincoln City's Sincil Bank ground, which was equidistance between Bradford and Norwich on the railway network. Usually such a game would have been staged at a football centre – Birmingham, Manchester or Sheffield – but due to the war 'quiet Lincoln' was selected. One gate would be open and a representative of each club would be on hand to decide whether potential attendees were 'fit and proper persons'. A large number of City supporters somehow found their way to Lincoln and around one hundred managed to convince those on the gate to allow them in. The oddity of the replay attracted a 'larger than usual gathering of the press'. Soldiers were admitted without question and they formed the bulk of the crowd. Throughout the first half a considerable number of people attempted to climb over the walls into the ground and at half-time the officials gave up and around five hundred gained admission.

The tie remained stubbornly scoreless until thirteen minutes from time. Peter Logan crossed, and Joe Lansdale in the Canaries net fell over, leaving Jimmy McDonald with the simple task of scoring from close range. Jimmy McIlvenny, back following his suspension, skimmed the bar before Jock Ewart made an outstanding save to protect City's lead. Norwich's brave resistance was ended when Dickie Bond converted a late penalty and Bradford City won 2-0. It was a remarkable FA Cup tie and possibly the strangest in the history of the competition. It was hardly the best preparation for the quarter final but at least City had home advantage.

So Valley Parade played host to another FA Cup quarter final. This time there was to be no repeat of the record crowd that had witnessed the 1911 quarter final with Burnley. There were no excursion trains to bring in the crowds from the surrounding district and this reduced the attendance to 26,100. All the quarter final ties suffered: the gate receipts at Valley Parade were £1,024; at Chelsea £1,800; Bolton £733; and Oldham £583. City's growing injury list and their exertions in the replays against Norwich told against them. The visitors Everton were being tipped to lift the trophy and the Bantams' rearranged forward line never threatened the visitors' defence. Jock Ewart

Jimmy McDonald

Dickie Bond, right, in a German prisoner of war camp in 1916

made some 'dazzling saves' to keep the score line respectable at 0-2 but inevitably the Bantams bowed out of the competition.

In Division One Liverpool were defeated by City in a rearranged midweek match, but a loss at relegation haunted Manchester United continued Bradford City's erratic form since the turn of the year. However, it was becoming apparent that football was unlikely to carry on beyond the end of the season. The war had ground to a bloody stalemate and the casualty figures were growing daily. When Bolton Wanderers visited Valley Parade on 20 March 1915 they wore black armbands in memory of Captain A V. Makent, the son of their club president, who had been killed in action. On the quarter hour James Marshall outpaced the Wanderers' defence and scored with a low shot to put City on their way to a 4-2 victory. Peter Currie, Jimmy McDonald and Jimmy McIlvenny completed the scoring. James Marshall scored in a single goal victory over Oldham Athletic. At Blackburn the following Saturday City's injured list was added to when Bob Torrance severely sprained his ankle and Peter Currie pulled a muscle. To add to the Bantams' woes, Rovers winning goal was a cross that was blown into the net by a strong gust of wind.

On 29 March 1915 the Football Association and Football League met to discuss the growing financial crisis in the game. They agreed to lower the players' maximum wage to £3 per week and abandon summer pay. The new rules would save City around £1,500 per year. There was also much discussion of the fact that of 1,800 professional footballers only 122 had enlisted for the armed forces. Frank Buckley, who had cost City a considerable transfer fee in the summer, had joined-up and was serving with the Footballers' Battalion. Bradford (Park Avenue) amateurs Donald Bell and Kirby had also enlisted.

The Bantams' form continued to baffle all. They lost 0-2 at Chelsea after George Waddell was sent off but then defeated Notts County 3-1. City suffered even more injuries when the league leaders Manchester City visited Valley Parade on 6 April. The visitors' striker Billy Jones clashed with Jock Ewart and the Bantams goalkeeper had to retire hurt. Jimmy McIlvenny took over in goal but he was also seriously injured following a collision with Jones! Despite the absentees City managed a goalless draw and then repeated the feat at Sunderland. Sheffield Wednesday were defeated 1-0 in the final home game of the season on 17 April 1915 in front of a mere ten thousand supporters. Five days later Harry Walden joined the Bradford Pals. Before becoming a professional footballer Walden had been a sergeant in the Cheshire Regiment and he had instructed the City players in military drill at the start of the war. On the same afternoon Walden joined up Dickie Bond also enlisted with the Bradford Pals. Bond had previously served in the army as a private in the Royal Artillery at Liverpool.

The final game of the season was the rearranged derby match at Park Avenue on Wednesday 28 April 1915. The *Bradford Daily Argus* carried full length portraits of Bond and Walden in their army uniforms. On the same page the sad news of the death of former City centre half Gerald Kirk was announced. He died of wounds sustained whilst leading his company into action in Belgium. What should have been one of the great moments in Bradford's sporting history was utterly overshadowed by the war. The kick off at Park Avenue was moved back to 6pm. It allowed thousands of workers in overalls to attend the match straight from their factories. A large

Gerald Kirk

proportion of the crowd were soldiers. Bradford took an early lead when McCandless and Jobey converged on Jock Ewart. The ball fell free and, as the Bradford City players appealed for a free kick, McCandless scored. Tommy Little extended Bradford's lead on twenty eight minutes and by half time City were three down: James Bauchop beat Joe Hargreaves, Irvine Boocock and drew Jock Ewart before scoring a tremendous goal. At half-time the twenty five thousand crowd listened to recruiting speeches. Captain Burton of the Bradford Pals held up the front page of the *Bradford Daily Argus* with the photographs of Bond and Walden. Dickie Bond himself donned his corporal's jacket to join his captain in appealing for new recruits.

The second half saw an improvement from City but the forwards were 'all over the place' and the game ended in a 0-3 reverse. The result left Bradford City in tenth place in the Division One table, immediately below Bradford (Park Avenue). The huge injury list after the turn of the year had robbed City of any chance of challenging for the Division One title and the gruelling replays against Norwich left the team jaded and unable to do themselves justice in the quarter final against Everton. The Bradford derby at Park Avenue was to be City's final Football League match for four long years. Their investment in attacking players in the summer of 1914 had increased the bank overdraft to £6,900. The club was reliant on the directors who guaranteed the overdraft and over the war years they would be indebted to the former Manningham player Arthur Lancaster. He became the club's chairman in 1917 and kept the club afloat during the Great War.

Nine current and former Bradford City players were killed in the conflict. The FA Cup winning captain and goalscorer Jimmy Speirs; the man of the match in the FA Cup final replay, Bob Torrance; the England midfielder Evelyn Lintott; City's first ever England international Jimmy Conlin; centre

half James Comrie; the amateur defender Gerald Kirk; and last but not least, reserves George Draycott, Ernest Goodwin and Harry Potter.

Dickie Bond laying a wreath at the Cenotaph in London in memory of his team mates killed in the Great War.

Several celebratory events took place to commemorate the FA Cup victory

Conclusion

Bradford City's promotion to Division One in 1908, a mere five years after the club's formation in 1903, which was then followed by the FA Cup triumph in 1911 represented a major achievement. This is particularly so when one considers that Bradford was a rugby stronghold and that schools football was the city's only real engagement with association football (or 'soccer') prior to the formation of Bradford City AFC. The men who transformed a failing rugby league club into a first division football club deserve to be remembered with pride and gratitude. People such as the club president Alfred Ayrton and the team manager Peter O'Rourke should be celebrated as much, if not more so, than the FA Cup final heroes Jimmy Speirs and Bob Torrance.

Like so many other members of the FA Cup winning team, Speirs and Torrance were Scotsmen and much comment has been made of this. However, their presence was unsurprising in that Bradford City were following a well trodden path. For example the famous Preston North End 'invincibles' team which won the FA Cup and League Championship double in 1888/89 was dominated by Scotsmen. The early development of professional football north of the border ensured that there was a ready supply of talent available to English clubs. Given the late adoption of football in Bradford there was bound to be a time lag before local footballers of sufficient talent would emerge. Allerton born Wally Smith was probably the first locally born player to appear for the Bantams in 1905 but the real breakthrough came when Cleckheaton born Irvine Boocock made his first team debut in March 1910. By then Bradford City were well on their way to establishing themselves as one of the leading clubs in the country; had it not been for the Great War it was widely accepted that Boocock would have received an England call up.

Although Bradford City's golden age took placing during an era when players were restricted to a maximum wage – a policy designed to make the Football League as competitive as possible – those clubs capable of attracting the largest attendances were able to lure the best talent by way of lucrative benefit matches. These were normal Football League matches but one where a qualifying player, usually defined by several years service to the club concerned, received the gate receipts. This placed clubs such as Aston Villa and Newcastle United at a great advantage as their regular forty thousand crowds could be used as an incentive to attract a player to sign on the dotted line. Bradford City were fairly generous when allocating benefit matches and, as their attendances were higher than the divisional average, the Bantams could often use the benefit match rules to their advantage. However, that advantage only existed as long as Bradford City retained their regional supremacy and continued to attract support from all parts of West Yorkshire. The rise of Bradford (Park Avenue), and after the Great War Huddersfield Town, threatened and eventually undermined that status.

The growing local competition for support, allied to a desire to repeat the success of 1911 and establish the club among the sport's elite, led to a decision to invest heavily in attacking players during the summer of 1914. Bradford City's defence was, by common consent, the best in the Football League and there was a real expectation that City could once again lift the FA Cup and make a sustained challenge for the Football League Championship. It was a huge gamble and, given the gathering war clouds, one that could hardly have been made at a more inauspicious moment. However, as the popular perception was that the war would be 'over by Christmas' there was no reason for the club to believe otherwise. Had the war lasted only a handful of months then its impact on football would have been as limited as conflicts that were fresh in the contemporary memory such as the Boer War. Had that been the case Bradford City would have been left in a very strong position. Sadly, the Great War was to become one of the greatest tragedies in European history but during the summer of 1914 how could the directors of Bradford City know that? It was undoubtedly a gamble, but was it any greater than the one the club had taken when it abandoned rugby in 1903 and joined the Football League without having kicked a ball?

The background to the investment decision was that Bradford City had remained loss-making in the three successive seasons from 1912/13 to 1914/15 despite having previously been profitable in each of its first four seasons in Division One (that is from 1908 to 1912). Ominously by 1915 the club had depleted its reserves and there had been a gradual increase in the club's overdraft which had been required to help fund the player signings. The club was not in a strong position to cope with a shut down during the Great War and ultimately relied upon Arthur Lancaster (director and former Manningham rugby player) as benefactor to survive.

Financial constraints had meant that the club had to maintain a finely balanced strategy. On the one hand it was one based on taking risks (at which it had been successful) but on the other there was also a deliberate policy of steadily reducing (or at least containing) the club's debts which were ultimately secured by director guarantees. Building a professional football club from scratch and developing a suitable ground on what was a challenging site (i.e. a hillside) represented a major financial commitment even in the era of the maximum wage. The club's shareholder capital base was low in comparison with its competitors and it was therefore reliant on gate receipts and/or debt finance. Progression in the FA Cup was thus vital and as we have seen, an early exit placed huge strain on the club's finances. Part of the club's problem was its origins: Bradford City AFC had evolved from a second rate rugby league team and one that had been firmly in the shadow of its cross-town rival Bradford FC. The Park Avenue club had historically been the 'city club' and that inevitably attracted money and the social elite. City's predecessors Manningham resented their second class status and had often presented themselves as the club of the working man. The identities that arose around late nineteenth century rugby in Bradford would hinder, and eventually fatally undermine, Bradford City's bid to establish themselves among the first division elite.

The rejection of the 1907 proposal that would have seen Bradford City move to Park Avenue and merge with their former rivals Bradford was a critical moment in the history of Bradford sport. The former Manningham faction among Bradford City's support dominated the debate about the merger proposal. Although they had legitimate concerns about the autocratic owner of Bradford FC Harry Briggs, the decision ultimately turned on identity. The former Manningham members were rightly proud of their achievements in forming Bradford City and as the debate raged City were building towards the team that would win the Division Two championship in 1907/08. However, it was their former Manningham identity and enmity towards the Bradford club that killed the merger. From a dispassionate viewpoint the merger made perfect sense. Bradford City had only a three month lease on Valley Parade so merging the established City team and utilising the superior facilities at Park Avenue was a logical step. The sticking point was the wealth and power of the Bradford directors and many City members feared that the merger was little more than a take over.

Of course, in the wake of the rejection Bradford City won the FA Cup and were regular contenders for the Football League championship. Even when Bradford (Park Avenue) FC achieved promoted to Division One there appeared to be little cause for concern. Many looked to other two club cities - such as Nottingham, Liverpool, Manchester and Sheffield - and noted the prestige that Bradford enjoyed by having two first division clubs. However the difference between Bradford and those cities was that football had been established a generation earlier and had no real additional competition from rugby. The following decades would prove the folly of dividing Bradford's support and financial capital between two Football League clubs and one Rugby League club. What amounted to little more than a petty localised rivalry condemned Bradford to sporting underachievement until a brief spell at the end of the century when City re-attained first division status in the Premier League and Bradford Bulls (nee Northern) achieved its own dominance of the RL Super League. Sadly, in both cases the success was short lived.

However, it would be churlish to conclude on a downbeat note. What a moment it must have been when the team returned to Bradford with the FA Cup on 26 April, 1911. A third of the entire population of the city packed onto the streets to witness Jimmy Speirs holding the glittering trophy aloft. It is that moment that has inspired generations to remain loyal to the club and provided credibility despite decades of underachievement. For whatever our current plight, we can proudly state that the name of our club, Bradford City AFC was the first on the most famous sporting trophy in the world.

It's Bradford's cup and it always will be!

The Cup Winners

Robert 'Bob' Campbell

Born Lugar Boswell in Scotland, Bob Campbell joined Partick Thistle as a 16-year-old. He made his debut a year later and won the second division title with Thistle. Representative honours followed when Campbell played for the Scottish League against their Irish counterparts at Belfast. Glasgow Rangers moved in for the emerging talent but after less than one season Campbell joined Millwall on a year's loan.

With several clubs looking to sign Campbell it took some enterprising work by Peter O'Rourke, and former Manningham player Ike Newton, to persuade the burly full back to sign for Bradford City in the summer of 1906.

In a long career at Valley Parade he won a Division Two Championship medal in 1908 and made nearly 250 appearances for the Bantams. Renowned for his hefty clearances, the popular full-back was one of the stars of the FA Cup triumph. On a tour of Belgium, the locals nicknamed him L'Aime, due to the fact he rarely had a smile off his face.

Bob was a fine all-round sportsman being a keen angler and a professional cricketer with the Clydesdale club. He retired to Scotland during World War One. He died in Ayr County Hospital in 1931, aged only 49.

Archie Devine

A Scottish midfielder, Archie played for Hearts, Raith Rovers and Falkirk before arriving at Valley Parade in 1910. Though he initially found the transition from Scottish to English football difficult, he soon found his feet and scored a brace at Manchester City in only his fifth first division match in November 1910. From then on he was a regular feature in the Bantams' midfield.

He made 60 appearances for the Bantams, scoring 11 goals - one of which was the vital second goal which broke Blackburn Rovers' challenge in the FA Cup semi-final. He played in all but one of the FA Cup matches during the unforgettable 1910/11 campaign and was a worthy member of the FA Cup winning side.

He joined Arsenal on 14 February 1913 for the then huge fee of £1,300. He later played for Shelbourne in southern Ireland, before returning to his native Scotland and Cowdenbeath. He ended his career where it began with his local side Lochgelly United. After retiring from the game he worked as a miner and dockyard worker at Rosyth. He was the last surviving member of the FA Cup winning side and died at Lochgelly in 1964, aged 78.

Peter Logan

Edinburgh born midfielder Peter Logan served Bradford City for seventeen years - all but three of which were in the first division. Though the Great War interrupted his career, he made 304 appearances for the club, either side of the conflict.

Logan joined City from Edinburgh amateur club St Bernards in 1908. Though the undoubted highlight of his career was the FA Cup victory, Logan's 43 goals from midfield made him a favourite of the Valley Parade crowds. The partnership Logan struck up with Jimmy Speirs was one of the planks upon which City's golden age was built.

His final appearance for the Bantams was on 11 April, 1925 – astonishingly his debut had been on 24 October, 1908. Peter Logan became City's trainer when he hung his boots up. After retiring from the game he became the licensee of the Girlington Hotel. He died in the Toller Lane district of the city in 1944, aged 54.

Jimmy McDonald

A City scout was sent to watch a striker playing for Edinburgh club St Bernards. His eye strayed from his intended target and focused on inside forward Jimmy McDonald. The Scotsman signed in April, 1907.

At Valley Parade he linked up with forwards George Handley and Frank O'Rourke. The trio played a major part in securing the Division Two Championship in 1908. Between them they notched up 50 goals as City gained promotion to the top flight. However, Jimmy was not an out-and-out goalscorer. He was a great distributor of the ball and many of Handley's and O'Rourke's goals were provided by the cultured Aberdonian.

McDonald came perilously close to being banned for life by City's strict disciplinarian manager Peter O'Rourke after Jimmy had joined City's England international Dickie Bond on a wild night out at Otley in December 1910. Thankfully, O'Rourke relented.

Jimmy played in the FA Cup Final of 1911 and captained the side in the days leading up to the First World War. During the war he served in the Royal Field Artillery as a driver. After the conflict he never really recovered his form and in May, 1920 he signed for Raith Rovers. Sadly, before he had played a game he became ill and died in Batley hospital, aged just 40.

Mark Mellors

The tall goalkeeper Mark Mellors joined Bradford City from Sheffield United in March, 1909 for £350. He had previously played for his hometown club Notts County as well as Brighton & Hove Albion.

When Mark arrived at Valley Parade the club was fighting against relegation from Division One. He replaced Martin Spendiff in goal after which the Bantams underwent something of a revival. In the last game of the season City needed to defeat Manchester United to avoid the drop. Mark was the hero of the day as City won 1-0. In the closing minutes he was knocked out as he threw himself into the path of a vicious drive. He was propped against the goalpost as City defended the resulting corner and at the final whistle the crowd carried him shoulder high from the field. His greatest feat came during the FA Cup winning campaign of 1911 when he conceded only one goal.

Mark Mellors retired in 1918 but remained in Bradford as a successful businessman in the wool trade, forming the company Mellors, Munro & Co. He was a regular at Valley Parade until his death at his home at Tranmere Park, Guiseley in 1961 aged 81.

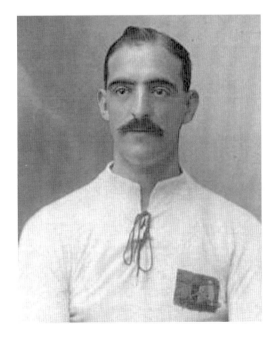

Glorious 1911 and Bradford City's Golden Age

Frank O'Rourke

A robust Scottish centre-forward, Frank O'Rourke had already won an international cap when he appeared at Valley Parade in April, 1907 playing in a friendly for Airdrie. He made such an impression that City officials travelled over to Airdrie's Leeds hotel, roused Frank from his bed at 3am, and signed him there and then!

He was an immediate success - his shoot on sight approach made him a favourite of the Valley Parade crowd. Frank became City's record scorer with 93 goals - a record only broken by Bobby Campbell in 1984. In the FA Cup Final replay of 1911 the press claimed that Frank touched Jimmy Speirs' header before it entered the net. However, he never claimed the goal and told his friends and family that he didn't make any contact.

At the outbreak of the First World War Frank O'Rourke drove a taxi in Bradford before joining the Royal Flying Corps. He retired in June,1926 and returned to Scotland and his native Bargeddie where he died on Christmas Eve, 1954 aged 77.

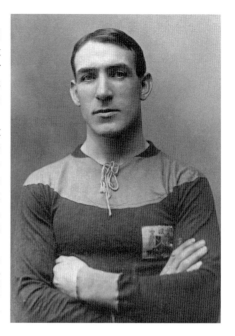

George 'Geordie' Robinson

'Geordie' Robinson's career spanned City's formation and golden age from the club's opening game through to the 1911 FA Cup Final and then relegation from the top flight.

Born at Basford, near Nottingham, in 1878 he played junior football with Basford Wanderers,

Notts Jardines and Newark before signing for Nottingham Forest. He appeared for Forest in an FA Cup semi-final against Southampton in 1898. George also played baseball for Nottingham and was a member of the team that won the English Baseball Cup.

Robinson came to Valley Parade from Nottingham Forest in June, 1903. He played in City's first ever match at Grimsby on 1st September, 1903. He went on to captain the side to the second division championship in 1908 and was vice-captain when City won the FA Cup in 1911.

After the First World War George Robinson retired to become City's trainer. It was a position he held until City's relegation from Division One in 1922 and in his 19-year association with the club he achieved 377 appearances and 19 goals. George was an unfussy half-back who was well regarded by the Valley Parade crowds. Despite being a native of Nottingham, he remained in Bradford after leaving the club and worked in a garage near Valley Parade. He was a regular supporter till his death aged 67 on 11th March, 1945.

Jimmy Speirs

Jimmy Speirs will forever be remembered as the man who captained Bradford City and scored the winning goal, during the 1911 FA Cup Final replay. His name has become synonymous with the golden age of the club and one hundred years later he remains the icon of the cup winning team.

James Hamilton Speirs was born in Glasgow in 1886. A natural striker, he played for Glasgow Rangers and Clyde, winning a Scottish cap in 1908. He signed for Bradford City in July, 1909 and captained the side, playing in 86 League games and scoring 29 times. His career peaked when he scored the winning goal in the 1911 FA Cup final replay at Old Trafford.

In December,1912 Jimmy was sold to Leeds City for a reported fee of £1,400 – a huge amount at a time when the national average wage was just £2 per week. At the outbreak of the Great War, Jimmy returned to his native Glasgow and enlisted in the Cameron Highlanders. He was awarded the Military Medal for bravery in May 1917 and promoted to Sergeant. He was killed during the notorious battle of Passchendaele on 10th August, 1917. Jimmy is buried at Dochy Farm New British Cemetery, near Ypres in Belgium.

David Taylor

Another Scot, David Taylor joined Bradford City from Glasgow Rangers in 1910. Taylor was at Valley Parade for barely a year but in that time City changed him from a forward to a top class defender.

He made 51 appearances for the Bantams, but only seven months after the FA Cup final he joined Burnley for a large fee. Apparently his wife had never taken to life in Bradford and Taylor himself disliked the city. At Turf Moor he won the League Championship and another FA Cup winner's medal in 1914.

Taylor returned to his native Scotland at the end of his playing career where he became manager of St Johnstone and later Dunfermline. He came back to England to take charge of Carlisle United before retiring to Perth in 1939. He died at Bridge of Allen in 1950.

Frank Thompson

An Irish midfielder, Thompson had already won the Irish League Championship and two Irish Cup finals with Cliftonville before arriving at Valley Parade in 1910, via Everton.

Frank scored vital goals on the way to the capture of the FA Cup. He headed the winner that defeated Burnley in the quarter-final at Valley Parade in front of a record 39,146 crowd. He also scored in the semi-final against Blackburn Rovers.

Thompson stayed at Valley Parade only three years, but won seven Irish caps during that time. He departed for Clyde in 1913 where he eventually became their player-manager. Frank later managed Irish club Glentoran. He died in Ayr County Hospital in 1950.

Robert 'Bob' Torrance

Born 1888 in Kirkintilloch, north-east of Glasgow. Bob Torrance joined City for a mere £5 from hometown team Kirkintilloch Harp in August, 1908. He made his debut on 28 November, 1908

R. TORRANCE
BRADFORD CITY F.C.

against Everton at Valley Parade. Though initially a full back, it was in central defence where he made his name.

Bob replaced William Gildea for the FA Cup Final replay against Newcastle United in 1911. He had a magnificent game and was widely acclaimed as the man-of-the-match. He went onto establish himself as one of the finest centre-backs in the land. He played two international trial matches for Scotland in 1913 and 1914 when the 'Anglo-Scots' took on the 'Home-Scots'.

Bob married a local butcher's daughter at Bradford Cathedral in 1916 and set up home on Wakefield Road. His final appearance for City was in a War League game against Barnsley on 10 March, 1917. Later that month he enlisted at the recruiting office on Bridge Street. He became a gunner with the 162nd Royal Field Artillery. Robert was killed during the Germans' last all-or-nothing offensive on 24th April 1918. Sadly, he has no known grave and is commemorated on the Tyne Cot Memorial to the Missing near Ypres, Belgium.

Willie Gildea

Born Broxburn, near Falkirk in 1888. A centre half, he joined City from Falkirk in February, 1911.

Willie spent an unhappy seven months at Valley Parade, making only ten appearances – three of which were in the cup run and included the final itself at the Crystal Palace. He was dropped for the FA Cup final replay which only intensified his disquiet.

Not surprisingly, he was the first of the cup winning squad to leave when he joined Birmingham City in September, 1911. His transfer fee was reported as 'nearly £1,000'. Gildea had developed tremendously under the tutelage of trainer Charlie Harper. It was said that 'whilst he would never be a racehorse, he is very clever, a beautiful feeder and a pretty weighty fellow'. Apparently, he was a musician and often entertained his fellow players whilst coming home from away games. He went onto Belfast Celtic before retiring from football. Willie died at Edinburgh in 1949.

Players who appeared in preceding rounds
Richard 'Dickie' Bond

'Dickie' Bond was one of City's greatest, albeit most controversial, players. When he came to Bradford City from Preston North End in May, 1909 he had already been capped by England and had established himself as one of the finest wide players in the country.

He became a key member of City's golden age side and added more England caps whilst at the club. However he was dropped for the 1911 FA Cup Final following a suspension after using 'improper language' to the crowd at Arsenal. Dickie's suspension from 8 March-8 April prevented him playing in the quarter and semi-finals. Though he returned to League action, manager Peter O'Rourke kept faith with the side that had got City to the final. Whilst Dickie travelled to the Crystal Palace and the replay at Old Trafford as one of four named reserves, he never made the team.

It was to be the one great regret of Bond's career but his antics at Arsenal were not the first time that he had found himself incurring the wrath of the disciplinarian O'Rourke. Only a year earlier Dickie had been suspended following a 'wild night out' in Otley during December, 1910 with Jimmy McDonald and Robert Campbell.

At the outbreak of the First World War Bond joined the Bradford Pals. During the half-time interval of his last peacetime match for City – at Park Avenue on 28 April, 1915 – he donned his corporal's uniform and made an appeal for volunteers. Dickie served as a machine gunner at the battle of the Somme in 1916. Later in the War he was taken prisoner at Neuve Chapelle. The Pals had barely taken over the sector when a German raid killed over sixty men and captured several others. Dickie was shaving when the Germans entered the trench and was caught completely unawares. The following night the Germans placed a sign in no-mans land welcoming the Bradford Pals to the front and sarcastically asking the whereabouts of Dickie Bond. He spent two years as a POW but within days of his release he turned out for City in a Bradford derby at Valley Parade.

Following the Bantams' relegation from the top flight in 1922, Dickie was transferred to Blackburn Rovers. After a long career he left the game to run a fish and chip shop in his native Garstang and later became a publican. He died aged 77 at Preston on 25th April, 1955.

George Chaplin

Another Scot, born Dundee in 27 September, 1888. A hugely popular right back, he joined City in October 1908 from Dundee. George made 97 appearances for the Paraders. He played in the first and second rounds of the Cup run before a bout of tuberculosis forced a lengthy absence from the game. George guested for Hull City during World War One and after the conflict he joined Coventry City in May 1919. He died on 14 May, 1963.

Harry Hampton

An Irish left half, he joined Bradford City from Dundee in March, 1910. Harry had much success with Aston Villa where he had already won the FA Cup. However, he never really rediscovered the form he had shown at Villa Park. That said, whilst at Valley Parade he made nine appearances for Ireland. In the 1910/11 FA Cup run Harry played in the second round against Norwich City. He turned out 50 times for the Paraders before joining Belfast Distillery in May, 1914.

James Blair

Dumfries born half-back. James began his career at Maxwell Town Volunteers and came to Valley Parade in May, 1910 via Kilmarnock and Manchester City. James played in only the first round at New Brompton (now Gillingham). He made 42 appearances for Bradford City, scoring 4 goals before joining Stockport County in August, 1912. He retired from County and returned home to Dumfries. On 26 March, 1913 he committed suicide when he cut his own throat in the family toilet.

Henry Peart

Born Newcastle 1889, Harry Peart was a centre half who joined Bradford City from Glasgow Strathside in June, 1909. Henry played in the second round against Norwich City. He made only 14 appearances for the Paraders before his transfer to Leeds City in September, 1913.

Postscript – More pain than glory

1915-2011

David Markham

Winning the FA Cup and finishing fifth in the top division has been the best Bradford City have been able to manage in their 108 year history.

True. City managed to extend their top division status for another nine years after the cup triumph, including four years when the League programme was suspended because of war, but for most of their long history their supporters have had to be content with a diet of lower division football.

Clearly, mistakes on and off the field have contributed to that, but the running theme in their history has been a lack of investment to compete with cities of a similar size. The likes of Nottingham, Coventry and Leicester, not to mention smaller places like Blackburn, Burnley and Bolton have all enjoyed greater success on the football field over the years than Bradford City.

Various changes were made after the cup final triumph as City settled into a mid-table position in the first division leading up to the First World War. However, when League football resumed after a four-year gap, City found themselves with a team that was growing old and ultimately were unable to bring in younger players to match the club's pre-war heroes. As well as that, the war had put the club under even greater financial pressure and it was only through the financial support of director Arthur Lancaster that they

survived. Bradford City clung on to their first division status for another three years after the war, but manager Peter O'Rourke left in 1921 and the following season they were relegated under new manager David Menzies after an extraordinary end-of-season collapse when they lost their last five matches after being in a seemingly safe position.

Menzies was unable to replace the fine players who had won the cup and kept City in the first division for 11 years after that. Consequently the supporters had to settle for a diet of lower, mid-

table second division football. Not surprisingly, City decided not to renew the contract of Menzies when he had completed five years as manager and chose in his place the intellectual Colin Veitch, who had faced City in the 1911 final during an illustrious career with Newcastle. Outstanding though he had been as a player, Veitch was a failure as a manager at Valley Parade and City finished bottom as they were relegated to the recently formed Division Three (North) in his first season. They recovered some pride by finishing sixth in his second campaign, but by then the club faced a serious financial crisis. The players left at the end of the season without having had

their wages paid which required generous donations by supporters and a three-day fund-raising bazaar in October, 1927. A re-constructed board, master minded by Tom Paton, who had been an instrumental figure behind the scenes at Valley Parade in the early years of the club, saved the day.

The legendary Peter O'Rourke then returned as manager and led them to the Division Three (North) championship in 1928/29 with a record number of goals: 128 from a 42 match programme and a goal difference of +85 with inspired signing Bert Whitehurst scoring a remarkable 24 in 15 appearances. O'Rourke left the club for the last time after City narrowly survived relegation in their first season back in the second division.

Mistakes made in the 1930s condemned the club to lower division football for 48 years. Respected manager Jack Peart, who took charge after succeeding O'Rourke, proved to be a good judge of players and a team builder as he gradually rejuvenated the championship winning team and then came a critical moment. In the middle of the 1932/33 season City were well placed to make a realistic promotion challenge after winning eleven and losing only three matches at the halfway mark of the 21 match second division programme. However, the board were divided and they failed to make the two signings Peart had earmarked to strengthen the squad and the chance was gone. City collapsed in the second half of the season, winning only three matches after the halfway mark and finished a disappointing 11th.

They fared better the following campaign, finishing in sixth place, but by then the team had begun to break up. Notable departures were left back Sam Barkas, one of City's best ever players, who was sold to Manchester City for £5,000, reportedly so the club could pay the close season wages, and his full back partner Charlie Bicknell to West Ham two years later. Perhaps the most important departure of all, however, was Peart himself. The directors decided not to renew his contract in 1935 after five years at the club and replaced him with former Leeds United manager Dick Ray. It proved to be a bad move for, although Ray built a new team as he went back to Leeds for some of his signings, the standard of football went down and he couldn't prevent City from dropping back into the third division in 1937. Little did supporters realise that it would be another 48 years before City would regain their second division status.

Once it became clear that Bradford City would not be among the promotion candidates in their first season back in Division Three (North), Dick Ray left the club to be replaced by the experienced Fred Westgarth, who left his job as manager of Carlisle United to take charge at Valley Parade. In his first full season City finished a promising third, but only three matches were played in the following campaign, 1939/40 before war was declared. Westgarth left for Hartlepool during the war and director Bob Sharp, the head of a Bradford furnishing company, managed the club for three years before League football resumed in 1946.

Perhaps City directors felt they needed to sell the likes of Barkas to raise much needed cash. Whatever the reason no club that sells its best players can hope to prosper and, so, in the 1930s City not only missed the chance to make a serious challenge to return to Division One, but also lost the opportunity to establish themselves as a good class second division club, which later generations would have appreciated. We know from Bradford City's recent history with three relegations in six years in the first decade of the new century that it is much easier to go down than go back up.

Despite their third placed finish in the last season before the war, Bradford City were not in good shape when League football resumed in 1946/47 for only a handful of pre-war players were available and the club were forced to experiment with lots of new players, some of them local amateurs. Despite attracting five figure gates in the post war boom, City were forced to seek re-

election in 1948/49 when they used a then record number of 40 players and only narrowly avoided the same fate the following season.

The club tried a variety of managers, former England international defender Jack Barker, their first player-manager Jack Milburn, the experienced David Steele and then a high profile player-manager, Ivor Powell. The former Welsh international half back used to dominate the game from his midfield role, but was guilty of signing too many older players and the club made little or no progress during his two and a half years in charge. His main influence was on the field and, when his playing career was brought to a premature end with a bad knee injury six weeks into the 1954/55 season, his influence diminished and he left the club six months later.

His successor, the experienced Peter Jackson, who brought his 18-year-old twin sons, David and Peter with him from Wrexham, brought stability to the club during his six years in charge. However, although he signed goalscoring centre forwards, John McCole, Derek Stokes and David Layne as well as other fine players like John Reid, Bobby Webb and Tom Flockett, City never threatened to break out of the lower divisions. Nevertheless, they managed to finish third in 1957/58 and so earned a place in the new national third division – the top 12 from the two regional third divisions formed Division Three, the bottom 12 Division Four. The Jackson era will be remembered chiefly for two outstanding cup runs. The first ended in a fourth round defeat at Preston in 1958/59 and 12 months later they beat first division Everton at Valley Parade on the way to a fifth round home tie match against Burnley. The match against a side that won the first division championship that season created intense interest. City drew 2-2 at Valley Parade after leading 2-0 in front of a capacity 26,227 crowd before crashing out of the competition 0-5 in a replay at Turf Moor. The replay attracted a crowd of 52,850 with an estimated twenty thousand, many of them City fans, locked out of the ground.

The Burnley cup matches proved to be the high points of the Jackson era. City's League form

slumped after their cup exit and it wasn't until mid-season that he was able to replace Stokes, who had left for Huddersfield Town in a £20,000 deal in the summer after scoring 35 League and cup goals. Then Jackson signed David Layne from Swindon for £6,000. Unfortunately for him, that signing came too late to save his job as he was sacked three months later when relegation threatened.

Bradford City, who were relegated back to the fourth division at the end of that 1960/61 season, took their long suffering followers on a roller coaster journey through the 1960s. The decade began with relegation and ended with promotion with three promotions near misses and two re-election applications in between. Valley Parade life was certainly not dull in those days.

Jackson's successor the experienced Bob Brocklebank, the former Burnley player, who later managed Chesterfield, Birmingham City and Hull City, led City to two fifth placed finishes in Division Four with a re-election application sandwiched in between. The two near misses came in 1961/62 – Brocklebank's first season at the club – and 1963/64, both the result of second half revivals after poor results in the first half of the season. 'Bronco' Layne led City's promotion charge in the spring of 1962, breaking the club record with 34 League goals, but they just missed out on promotion after the poor start to the season left them too much to do.

Inevitably, Layne left during the summer, joining first division Sheffield Wednesday for £20,000 and he scored freely for Wednesday at the top level before being caught up in the betting scandals of the mid 1960's and was jailed and banned from playing professional football.

The following season City had to apply for re-election for the second time in their history during one of the worst winters in modern times, but Brocklebank mounted a second promotion in the second half of the

1963/64 campaign with a new centre forward, the former Park Avenue and Halifax Town player Rodney Green, who scored 29 goals in 44 League appearances. Unfortunately, City's promotion effort was de-railed in the next to the last crucial home match against Workington. Whoever won the match would gain promotion and a near capacity crowd of 17,974 gathered to witness what could have been a promotion celebration. However, City failed to rise to the big occasion and went down 0-2. Green left for Gillingham in a £7,000 deal that summer and, after a bad start to the new season, Brocklebank resigned.

Bradford City signed Welsh international Bill Harris from Middlesbrough as player manager to replace him and he guided the club to safety after they had been threatened with having to seek re-election again. The following season there was a change in the boardroom that would have significant implications for the next 20 years. City had won only two of their first 11 matches in 1965/66 and their eight defeats included successive 1-7 thrashings against Crewe away and

Stockport at home. Chairman Albert Harris, a local timber merchant, was at the end of his tether when Bradford toy manufacturer Stafford Heginbotham took over the club with his friend David Ide in October, 1965. Heginbotham, full of original ideas on how to market the club, immediately injected some much needed cash for new signings with Welsh international centre forward Ken Leek, who joined City from Northampton for a club record £10,000, the most eye catching newcomer. Unfortunately, neither Leek nor any other of the signings, including the return of Derek Stokes from Huddersfield could prevent City from having to seek re-election for the third time.

After Bill Harris, Heginbotham turned to double soccer and cricket international Willie Watson as manager, but he resigned after 18 months to be succeeded by Grenville Hair, the former Leeds United full back, who had left Elland Road to become player manager of Wellington Town, now AFC Telford. Tragically, Hair collapsed and died during a training session at Valley Parade in March, 1968 after only six weeks in charge. Again City missed out on promotion with a fifth placed finish and during the summer they turned to Reading assistant manager Jimmy Wheeler and former long serving player at the club as their new manager. Wheeler succeeded where his predecessors had failed, leading City to promotion after a thrilling finish to the season. At the halfway stage of the season, promotion looked to be a distant prospect, but City

went on a 21-match unbeaten run, which left them needing to win their last match of the season at promotion rivals Darlington.

Bradford City, who lasted three seasons in the third division, missed a great chance to gain promotion for the second season in a row. They were in a strong position in January, 1970 but fell

away badly. Stafford Heginbotham's board decided to raise some much needed cash for team strengthening by selling Valley Parade to Bradford Council for £35,000 and renting it back at ten per cent of the purchase price - £3,500 per year. Unfortunately, the two players Wheeler bought with the money, strikers, Colin Hall, £10,000 from Nottingham Forest and Michael Owen's father, Terry Owen, £7,000 from Everton were not successful singings and another chance of progress was wasted. Wheeler lost his job a month into the 1971/72 season and his successor, the former Bolton FA Cup winner, Bryan Edwards, who was

assistant manager at Plymouth when he joined City, could not save them from relegation.

After relegation, City became a mid-table fourth division club despite changes in the boardroom. Local businessman Bob Martin, who joined Heginbotham's board in 1972 became chairman the following year after recruiting Bradford supermarket magnate Ken Morrison as a director, but the effect of Morrison's involvement in the club appeared to be minimal to most supporters. After two and a half years, Bryan Edwards gave way in January, 1975 to youth team coach, Bobby Kennedy, the former Kilmarnock and Manchester City player, who also had a spell as player manager of Grimsby Town. During his three-year spell as manager Kennedy guided City to the quarter final of the FA Cup for the first time for 56 years and to promotion in successive seasons. They lost 0-1 to eventual FA Cup winners Southampton in front of the BBC Match of the

Day cameras at Valley Parade in March, 1976 and the following season they were promoted to the third division after finishing in fourth place in Division Four. Unfortunately there were insufficient funds for much needed team strengthening and City found the demands of the third division too much for them. So, they were relegated at the end of the season with Kennedy losing his job in the January.

Former Northern Ireland and Bolton defender, John Napier, one of Bryan Edwards' signings, succeeded Kennedy, but he lasted only months and City turned to the experienced George Mulhall,

the former Aberdeen and Sunderland winger, who had helped Bolton to promotion to the first division as assistant to former Huddersfield manager Ian Greaves. Mulhall introduced a constructive passing style of football at Valley Parade during his only full season as manager as City went agonisingly close to promotion in a dramatic and bitterly disappointing end to the 1979/80 campaign. They went into their last match at Peterborough needing only to draw to make sure of fourth place, but they went down 0-1 while four other results went against them.

The following season was an anti-climax as if the disappointment of missing out on promotion hung over the club like a cloud and Mulhall returned to Bolton two months before the end of the campaign, which led to an inspired appointment by Bob Martin. The chairman made Derby's former England defender Roy McFarland their player manager and, under his charismatic leadership on and off the field, City gained promotion as runners-up to champions Sheffield United.

Northern Ireland striker Bobby Campbell, who briefly resurrected his international career at the end of season on McFarland's recommendation after he had been banned for misbehaviour as a 17-year-old, was top scorer with 27 League and cup goals. City also equalled a club record nine

match winning run in the first half of the campaign. McFarland was the manager, who gave inspirational midfield player, Stuart McCall his debut at the start of the following season and the Bantams were just establishing themselves back in the third division when McFarland and his No 2 Mick Jones shocked everyone by walking out on the club to return to Derby as part of a new look management team involving Brian Clough's former assistant Peter Taylor. City were awarded £55,000 after Derby were found guilty of enticing McFarland to break his contract, but his departure had

little effect on the club thanks to another shrewd managerial appointment by Bob Martin. The City chairman tempted another former England defender, Trevor Cherry to leave Leeds United to become player manager and, with assistant, former Elland Road team mate Terry Yorath, an

inventive and inspirational coach, they guided the club into a mid-table position in their first season back in Division Three before a financial crisis struck in the summer of 1983.

There were signs of an impending crisis as soon as the 1982/83 season ended with various factions looking to take control of the club and then, at the end of June, it was announced that the club had been placed into receivership. Bob Martin stood down as chairman and the rest of the board resigned and the future of the club hung in the balance during that summer as various groups held talks with the receiver, Bradford accountant Peter Flesher to convince him they had the credentials and the necessary finance to take over the club. Eventually, two former directors, Stafford Heginbotham and Jack Tordoff came together to rescue the club with Heginbotham taking the chairmanship for a second time and Flesher also joining the board.

Money was understandably tight as City made a dreadful start to the new season, winning only one of their first 15 matches, but then Bobby Campbell, whom Peter Flesher had sold to Derby just before the season began for £70,000 to raise some much needed cash, returned after an unsuccessful spell in the Midlands and his return sparked a dramatic revival. City established a new club record by winning ten matches in a row and eventually finished a creditable seventh. That revival plus the key signings of winger John Hendrie and defender Dave Evans proved to be the inspiration for their third division championship campaign, bringing to an end 48 years of lower division football at Valley Parade. After a good start to the season, City went top with a 3-1 home win against Millwall at the end of November, 1984 and stayed there, making sure of the title with a 2-0 win at Bolton in the next to the last match of the season.

Disaster struck during that fateful final match against Lincoln City on 11 May, 1985. Captain Peter Jackson led the players on a lap of honour after being presented with the third division championship trophy before the match. Then, as half time approached, fire broke out in the main stand and spread rapidly. In just four minutes, the stand that had been constructed in 1908 (in preparation for first division football) was destroyed, 56 people had lost their lives and hundreds were injured. The story of one of Britain's worst football disasters was recalled in detail

during the moving commemoration events to mark the 25th anniversary of the tragedy in May, 2010. As far as the football club was concerned, the newly promoted team faced the demands of the second division without a ground of their own and no money to spend on team strengthening. Bradford Council were keen for the club to play at Odsal Stadium, the home of Bradford Northern Rugby League Club, which had been re-furbished for the world speedway championships while the directors also wanted them to play in Bradford. However, early matches were played at Leeds United and Huddersfield Town before Odsal was ready to stage League football. More matches were played at Leeds and Huddersfield later in the season as bad weather ruled out play at the exposed Odsal Stadium, but despite all these handicaps City finished a creditable 13th in the table.

After much deliberation, it was decided to re-build Valley Parade. The £2.6 million project was completed in six months and the ground was re-opened on an emotional afternoon in December, 1986 when the then England manager, Bobby Robson brought an England side, containing Peter Shilton and Kevin Keegan, flying specially from Spain to play City.

Sadly, City sacked Cherry a month later in the wake of some poor results and appointed

assistant manager Terry Dolan in his place. Dolan, a former City player, was a surprise appointment to some – Martin O'Neill also applied for the job – but it proved to be a good appointment because Dolan steered City to safety that season before preparing for a strong promotion challenge in the following campaign. He made two key signings – defender Lee Sinnott for a record £147,000 from Watford and goalkeeper Paul Tomlinson for £40,000 from Sheffield United. City began well with ten wins out of their first 13 matches, survived a mid-season blip and, with a week to go, they occupied the second automatic promotion place, but they lost their last two matches and had to settle for a play-off place. Middlesbrough beat them in the two-legged play-off semi-final and the chance of returning to the top division was gone. Even now, supporters still argue about how City missed out on automatic promotion and whether the team ought to have been strengthened in the last two months of the campaign as Dolan wanted.

The fall out from Bradford City's failure to gain promotion was to lose their two best players – Stuart McCall went to Everton for £850,000 and John Hendrie to Newcastle for £500,000. Chairman Jack Tordoff, who had succeeded Stafford Heginbotham six months earlier, had promised Dolan he could use this money on team strengthening. Dolan signed several new players, including future manager, striker Paul Jewell from Wigan for £80,000 and he also brought back defender and former captain Peter Jackson from Newcastle for £290,000. Jackson's return was not a success and he left two years later to revive his career at Huddersfield Town. Despite beating first division clubs, Tottenham Hotspur in the FA Cup and Everton in the League Cup, League form was inconsistent and Dolan and his assistant Stan Ternent were sacked at the end of January, 1989 after City had been knocked out of both cups in the space of a fortnight.

Tordoff decided to bring back former assistant manager Terry Yorath from Swansea to succeed Dolan although City were fined for making an illegal approach. Like Dolan, Tordoff allowed Yorath to spend freely and he brought in several new players like Jimmy Quinn, Mark Aizlewood, Alan Davies, Tony Adcock and Ian McCall, some for six figure fees, but his second spell at Valley Parade was not a success and, when Tordoff sold the club to a consortium headed by Bradford travel agent David Simpson in February, 1990, the former Welsh international's days were numbered. In fact, his 13 month spell as manager came to an end in March 1990 six weeks after Simpson took charge with relegation looming and City turned to a completely different type of manager as his successor, former Millwall boss John Docherty who had won the second division championship with Millwall two years earlier, the year City missed out on promotion. Docherty favoured the direct, long ball style of football whereas Yorath was a disciple of the close passing game. The new manager wasn't able to save City from relegation and proved to be highly unpopular with supporters during his eighteen months in charge. The fans hated his style of football and, when it became clear Docherty's methods were not proving to be effective the directors had no option but to terminate his contract.

Docherty's successor, former Arsenal and Manchester United striker Frank Stapleton was hampered by lack of funds in the transfer market as City showed no sign of a speedy return to the second division and, when they just failed to make the play-offs in 1993/94, new chairman Geoffrey Richmond called time on his two and half year spell at Valley Parade. Richmond, who swapped his position as chairman of Scarborough with Simpson and some other members of the City board moving in the other direction, proved to be arguably the most significant – and controversial – figure in Bradford City's modern era.

Richmond, who began by loaning the club £2 million to wipe off its debts as well as providing money for team strengthening, replaced Stapleton with the highly experienced Lennie Lawrence, the former long serving Charlton manager, who had not had his contract renewed after three years as Middlesbrough boss. Richmond provided considerable funds to be

spent in the transfer market, including record signing John Taylor, a £300,000 signing from Bristol Rovers, but Lawrence failed to find a consistent winning formula and after 18 months he gave way to his assistant and first signing Chris Kamara.

Kamara's appointment turned out to be a masterstroke by Richmond for, after a difficult first three months, the current Sky TV football commentator and presenter guided City to the play-offs with a consistent spell of results in the last three months of the 1995/96 season. City made sure of sixth place with a tense 3-2 win at Hull in the final match of the season, overcame a 2-0 home deficit to beat Blackpool 3-2 in the play-off semi-final on a memorable night at Bloomfield Road before winning promotion by beating Notts County in the play-off final in their first and only visit to Wembley Stadium to the delight of thirty thousand City supporters. Des Hamilton and Mark Stallard were the scorers in a remarkably comfortable win on a never to be forgotten day for the Bantams.

Kamara guided City to second division survival the following season thanks to an unprecedented influx of foreign players, a four-month spell from former England winger Chris Waddle and crucial wins in the last two matches of the season. However, City proved to be inconsistent in the following season and, in January 1998, Richmond controversially sacked Kamara and replaced him with coach Paul Jewell, which proved to be another inspired appointment.

The Bradford City management believed that the club had a good chance of gaining promotion to the Premier League the following season and, on this rare occasion in their history, the club had the money to back their ambitions – serious money, in fact. Julian Rhodes and his father Professor David Rhodes provided the money and an unprecedented spending spree led to promotion. City signed their first £1 million player, striker Lee Mills and two others followed, fellow striker Isaiah Rankin and later striker Dean Windass, but the most significant signing was the return of Stuart McCall from Glasgow Rangers. McCall, who had left the club ten years earlier, proved to be an inspirational captain as City made sure of the second automatic promotion place with an exciting and memorable 3-2 win at Wolves in the final match of the 1998/99 season with goals from Lee Mills, Peter Beagrie and Robbie Blake.

Now, came the task of staying in the Premier League. Jewell's key close season signing was defender David Wetherall, who cost a club record £1.4 million when he joined City from Leeds United and he is still with the club as head of youth. Bradford City gained their first Premier League win at Middlesbrough in the opening match of the season, but they understandably struggled for most of the campaign before ensuring their survival with a 1-0 home win against Liverpool in the final match, Wetherall heading the vital goal. Paul Jewell stunned supporters by resigning in the summer after differences with Geoffrey Richmond became clear and it's fair to say the club has gone downhill ever since his departure.

Richmond made another internal appointment, assistant manager Chris Hutchings succeeding Jewell and the club embarked on what has been dubbed the summer of madness with an even

more ambitious spending spree than two years earlier when they decided to challenge for the Premier League. City paid a club record £2.5 million for Leeds United midfield player David Hopkin, £1.5 million for Blackburn striker Ashley Ward and £1 million for Chelsea's Romanian midfield player Dan Petrescu, but the most controversial signing was Italian striker Benito Carbone on a reported £40,000 per week. Despite these signings, City made a bad start to the season, Hutchings lost his job in the November and new manager, Scot Jim Jefferies – who had just resigned as manager of Hearts – was not able to halt the decline.

So, City were faced with being back in the second division with a huge wage bill – a staggering £13 million in their second season in the Premier League. Petrescu had left to go to Southampton midway through the season, Hopkin had gone back to former club Crystal Palace and another high profile signing Stan Collymore had lasted only three months, but Carbone was still there (although he did have a spell on loan at Middlesbrough). Coupled with the high wage bill, there were payments for the £7.5 million main stand extension to manage. With little prospect of a speedy return to the Premier League, City parted company with Jim Jefferies at Christmas 2001. His replacement, Chesterfield manager Nicky Law guided City to safety and at the end of the season City supporters said farewell to their favourite son, McCall at a testimonial match against his former club Rangers which attracted a twenty-one thousand crowd to Valley Parade. McCall, who was not offered a new contract, joined Sheffield United. Off the field, however, the storm clouds were gathering and City went into administration. Excessive spending on players two years earlier, the money needed for the stand extension and the collapse of ITV Digital had all caught up on them as the club were reported to be £36 million in debt. Bradford City's future was in the balance through that anxious summer before the club received the clearance to start a new campaign two days before the first match. By this time, Geoffrey Richmond had left the club to be replaced by Gordon Gibb, owner of Flamingoland themepark with Julian Rhodes as chief executive and they guided the club through the 2002/03 season.

However, the club's centenary season proved to be a miserable affair. Nicky Law lasted only until the November of that season – he was sacked after City lost ten of their first 16 matches - and the directors then sprang a surprise by appointing the former England and Manchester United captain Bryan Robson as manager with former Bolton and Derby manager Colin Todd as his No 2. Todd, who like Robson had enjoyed an illustrious playing career with England as well as Sunderland and Derby had also spent six months as a coach at Valley Parade under Frank Stapleton. It seemed to be an impressive managerial pairing. Unfortunately, it wasn't. Four months after their appointment, City went into administration for a second time, Gordon Gibb resigned after apparent differences with the Rhodes family and some of City's best players - striker Andy Gray, young full back Simon Francis and Welsh international midfield Paul Evans - were sold to raise much needed cash. City were relegated and Bryan Robson decided not to continue as manager, leaving Colin Todd to hold the fort in the most difficult of circumstances. City came out of administration in the autumn of 2004 thanks to the generosity of the Rhodes family with Julian installed as chairman while Todd re-built his squad. In the circumstances, it was perhaps unrealistic to expect City to be serious promotion challengers. So, they settled into a mid-table team with the goalscoring exploits of Dean Windass being one of the few pleasures for City supporters. Windass, who had returned to the club from Sheffield United, was top scorer in four successive seasons in his second spell at Valley Parade and scored 28 goals in 2004/05 and 20 goals the following season.

Despite Windass's scoring feats Bradford City made little progress on the field and in January, 2007 – midway through Todd's third season – they allowed him to go on loan to his home town club Hull City. City saved money on his wages and also received a six-figure loan fee to help them to pay urgent bills. One month later – in February, 2007 – they sacked Colin Todd and installed David Wetherall as caretaker manager. Unfortunately, the move was not a success and how City missed Windass's goals as they slid towards relegation - back in the fourth tier of English football after a gap of 25 years.

Most City supporters always hoped that Stuart McCall would return as manager and so he received an ecstatic welcome when he returned from Sheffield United in May, 2007. Unfortunately, he was not able to achieve success as a manager and made a dignified exit in February, 2010 midway through his third season. Now, the club's immediate hopes on the field are pinned on his successor, the experienced Peter Taylor.

When City were formed in 1903, the wool trade was still buoyant and there were lots of wealthy woolmen, some of whom were interested enough to invest in the club, but the wool trade has declined considerably since the war along with manufacturing and the number of large locally owned firms in the city and surrounding district is small indeed. These changes in the local economy have all had a knock-on effect on the football club. Individuals such as Arthur Lancaster, Tom Paton, Bob Sharp, Stafford Heginbotham, Bob Martin, Jack Tordoff, Geoffrey Richmond and Julian Rhodes have been as important in determining the club's outlook in the various stages of its history as team managers themselves. Like Heginbotham, Tordoff, one of Yorkshire's most successful businessmen and the current club president, had two spells on the board and supported the club as a major sponsor after he ceased to be a director.

More recently, it has been the Rhodes family, who have carried the burden of guiding the club through two administrations that severely threatened its future existence. In the last three years Bradford businessman and lifelong fan, Mark Lawn has come forward to invest in City and share with Julian Rhodes in the running of the club, enjoying the title of joint chairmen. However, new investors are needed if the club is to progress in the modern era. Most supporters would settle for promotion back to the third division in the immediate future, but, a city the size of Bradford ought to be looking to running a successful second division side in the current Football League Championship with an outside chance of reaching the play-offs. For, even though the demographic nature of the city has changed considerably in the last forty years, the club's generous season ticket offer shows that the support is still there for a successful second tier team, but that will cost money and where are the local investors to make it happen?

David Markham is a journalist who has reported on Bradford City's affairs for various publications, including the Telegraph & Argus and the Press Association, for 36 years. A lifelong follower of the club he has also been involved in four books about Bradford City, the most recent of which was published in 2010.

CUP HEROES of OTHER DAYS
and WHAT HAS HAPPENED TO THEM

Eight Scots, two Nottinghamshire natives, and one Irishman, secured the greatest triumph in the history of Bradford football when, in a replayed final tie at Old Trafford in April, 1911, the City beat Newcastle United by an only goal. The members of that cosmopolitan company have met with varied fortunes and experiences in the intervening years, as this article will show.

AS the last line of defence, was a man who held a record probably equalised by no other goalkeeper either before or since, this being long and lanky **MARK MELLORS**, who was unbeaten in twelve successive cup-ties in that season and the following one. His great reach and agility made him one of the soundest goalkeepers the club ever had. He went to Valley Parade after extensive service with Notts County and Brighton and Hove Albion, and when he left City it was to retire from the game and settle in Bradford. In these days he is a smartly-dressed, well-groomed business man who is in the "piece" trade on his own account, and he is a regular attender at his old club's home matches.

Burly **BOB CAMPBELL** was one of the most vigorous right-backs of his day and a man who could balloon the ball as near to the skies as possible. There used to be some great duels between him and Arthur Bridgett of Sunderland. After leaving Partick Thistle, Glasgow Rangers, and Millwall, he first helped the Yorkshire club into the First Division before the cup triumph, and then remained with the club until the war which brought the end of his career in the field. He returned to his native Ayrshire, where he is a coal-miner.

A contrast and a foil to the vigorous Campbell was furnished by **DAVID TAYLOR**, one of the fastest backs the game ever knew. Previously a pivot with Glasgow Rangers and Motherwell, the City made a great discovery when they turned him into a back, for he was a skilled artist as well as a sprinter. Only for 14 months was he with the City, for he went to Burnley for a four-figure fee in December, 1911, and remained at Turf Moor until after the war, when he bade adieu to the playing arena and devoted his experience to managing St Johnstone, with which club he still holds the reins.

A persevering plodder who went about his work without fuss or flurry was **GEORGE ROBINSON**, who was the club's right half-back from its formation in 1903 until the outbreak of the war. A Nottingham native, the Forest was his only other League club, and George may be said to have been connected with the City almost

Bradford City (1911).

throughout its chequered history, for he fulfilled training duties at Valley Parade in later years, and to-day holds a responsible position in a Manningham garage almost within a stone's throw of the ground, at which, like Mellors, he is a frequent visitor.

Rufus-haired **BOB TORRANCE** is spoken of to this day as the subject of the happiest experiment Bradford City ever made. Another Scot who had had three seasons with the club as a reserve back after being secured from Kirkintolloch Rob Roy, it was a stroke of genius which led to the decision to play him at centre half-back in the replay after William Gildea had filled that role at Crystal Palace. Torrance was a wonderful success and the man of the match, his boundless energy and ruthless tackling cutting the Newcastle forward combination to shreds. Bob never kicked a ball for another League club, for he was at Valley Parade until the war, into which he went to fall in action in 1916 when in the prime of athletic manhood.

The cool and calculating craftsman of the middle line was **JIMMY McDONALD**, a Scot, who, after being recruited from Edinburgh St Bernard, was City's inside-left in a previous Second Division championship success. Then he devoted his artistry to the left half-back berth in which he remained chiefly until after the war. He, like Torrance, was attached to no other League club, and, also like his fellow-Scot, no longer is in the land of the living, for just when his playing days were at an end he died in hospital at Batley a few miles from Bradford.

Always smiling and always genial was **PETER LOGAN**, a skilful and resourceful light-weight who played all over the forward line, but was at outside-right in the final. He, like McDonald, was a Scot from Edinburgh St Bernard, and

host" of the Girlington Hotel, only about half a mile from Valley Parade.

The brains of the attack and the captaincy of the side rested with **JIMMY SPIERS**, a cultured scheming inside-right, but a quiet and reserved fellow who was a thinker rather than a talker. He made history by scoring the goal that won the cup. A Scottish International who had played with Rangers and Clyde when "with his ain folk," he left City to become commander-in-chief of the attack of the old Leeds City team, and that role he continued to fill until the war, in which he, like Torrance, was killed in action.

Bradford folks still say that City never had a centre-forward who could compare with **FRANK O'ROURKE**, who scored more goals for the club than any other player in its history. No relation of Peter, who, now, as then, is the City manager, Frank was robust, dashing, and utterly fearless, and delighted in a hefty shoulder charge, while his shooting was something out of the ordinary. He also helped City to promotion after becoming a Scottish International in his native land, where he was attached to Albion Rovers and Airdrieonians. He also finished his playing days with the club, which employed him as reserve team coach for some time after the war. To-day, he is working in his native Bargeddie. He was a bustler on the field, but as quiet and gentle as a mouse off it.

Still another Scottish International was at inside-left, this being **ARCHIE DEVINE**, who used to specialise in making the bullets for others fellows to fire. Raith Rovers, Hearts and Falkirk were Archie's clubs before he was brought over the Border, and his last English club was Arsenal, whom he joined from City. To-day he is employed at the docks in Glasgow along with William Gildea, who was City's pivot in the first final with Newcastle.

A "broth o' a bhoy" from Erin's Isle was the outside-left, and a fast, strong player, accurate in his crosses and a fine shot at goal was **FRANK THOMPSON**. He won every possible honour in his native Ireland, while helping Belfast Cliftonville, and City were lucky to get him after Everton had signed him as an amateur. After the cup conquest, Frank continued to be a City player for nearly three more seasons before he was transferred to Clyde, who, when his playing days ended, appointed him to the managerial post, so that he, like David Taylor, has charge of a Scottish League club.

Although **DICKY BOND** was not in the cup-winning team, he was a great favourite with the club's followers in those days, and for many years afterwards until he finished his career with Blackburn Rovers. He now has a fish and chip business at Garstang near his native Preston.

Three of the Bradford cup-winning team. Left to right—Peter Logan, Frank O'Rourke, and Mark Mellors.

Bradford suited him so well that it has been his home ever since he originally crossed the Cheviots. He was the utility man of City's attack right up to 1924, and then, after coaching the reserve team, he retired to become "mine

Another article in this series next week.

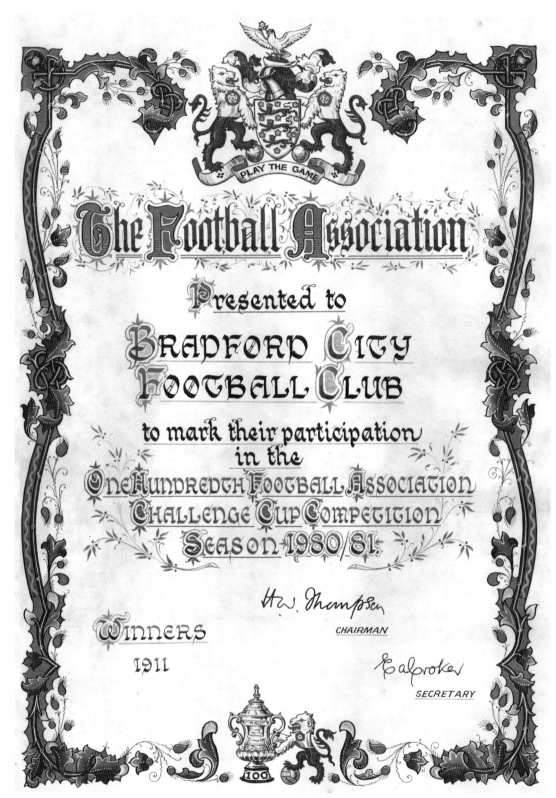

The Football Association

Presented to

Bradford City
Football Club

to mark their participation
in the
One Hundredth Football Association
Challenge Cup Competition
Season 1980/81.

Winners

1911

CHAIRMAN

SECRETARY

Certificate presented to Bradford City to mark their participation in the centenary season
of the FA Cup competition.

SUBSCRIBERS

The following subscribed to GLORIOUS 1911 in advance of publication and
we are grateful for their support.

Rosie Pendleton	Ian Bates	Darren Wilding
Neil Davies	Raymond Dawes	Ben Sykes
Brian Tewkesbury	Paul R.Smith	Malcolm Gardner
Kevin J. Antoncich	Andrew Norton	John C.Kermode
John E.J. Schofield-Antoncich	Chris Hawkridge	Peter Broscombe
Stephen Woodhouse	Paul Hawkridge	Keith B.Crowther
Tino Palmer	Mary Wallace	John A.W. Clough
Clive Palmer	Paul Jackson	Alan K. Biggin FCA
David Worsley	Paul Wood	Ian Hemmens
Martin K. Ham	Damian Light	Robert Hemmens
Rod Lawson	Sarah Dewhirst	Darren Slingsby
Peter M. Firth	Alison Dewhirst	Chloe Alice Ashcroft
Andrew N. Rawson	Emma Dewhirst	Benjamin Peter Ashcroft
Paul Martin Guest	Harry Dewhirst	Tom Stableford
Derek A. Vincent	Mary Dewhirst	Jeremy White
Andrew Sewell	Joanna Kingsley	Andy Stokes
Michael Pendleton	Wayne W. Head	www.jimmy-speirs.co.uk
Peter J. Mason	Peter Newsome	www.jimmy-speirs.co.uk
Alexander Jackson	Mike Harrison	Andrew D.Pickles
Darren Hird	Michael Levycky	Chris Overend
Julian Meekins	Edward Oliver	H. Glover
Oliver Donnelly	John R. Armitage	David Rhodes
Michael Crowther	Matthew Rishworth	Paul G. Collinge
Trond Langfjæran	Susan Gross	Steven Thurlby
John Cook	Johnathan Smith	Andrew Waller
Graham Walker	George Rishworth	Alix Oglesby
Mick Skelton	Eric R.Toulmin	Alan Hirst
Joe Skelton	Paul Dawson	John Beasty
Lee Skelton	David Burnet	Paul Firth
Mick Gibson	Graham Yaffe	David Firth
Richard Stretton	Graeme Wolfenden	C. Davidson
Rev. Malcolm Lorimer	Tony Lidgate	Jonathan Shepherd
Denis Graham Blyth	John Brewis	Alan Hirst
Robert Stuart Cummings	Catherine Mills	Eric Walker
Brian William Cummings	Alan Biggins	Benjamin Scott Cunliffe
Peter Jewitt	Paul Edgar Hughes	Sophie Hope Cunliffe
Colin Parker	Mohammed Ibrahim	Philip D. Clarke
Carl Hardy Barber	John Musgrave	Mathew Sutcliffe
Peter Knott	Richard Wardell	Alan Rhodes
Patrick Brady	Trevor Thomas	Chris Rhodes
Graham Hall	Peter Dolby	Mick Callaghan
Oscar Helliwell	Peter Sayer	Lottie Willis-Jump
Millie Helliwell	Tony Watson	Simon Andrew Scott
Zara Helliwell	James Lovedale	Lutz Tacke
Steven Lightowler	David King	Manny Dominguez
Jeff Spolnik	Chris Hodson	Steve Taylor
Evie Spolnik	Raymond G.Boyle	Alan Taylor
Mark R.Thornton	Richard and Sarah Johnston	Karen Taylor
Matilda Thornton	Dave Welbourne	Chris Pollard
David Storey	Chris Welbourne	Philip G. Artus
David Fenton	Alan Carling	
Adrian Calam	Craig Wilding	

Paraders

Retro Bradford City Badges

The PARADERS range of badges and cuff-links features historically authentic and long-forgotten designs including each of the crests and characters adopted by Manningham RFC and Bradford City AFC from the nineteenth century through to 1991. There is also a series of badges commemorating each of the club's promotion seasons (which are available to buy individually) as well as the rivalry with Bradford (PA) up to 1970.

This is an initiative in conjunction with the bantamspast museum at Valley Parade. Profits will be used to invest in new display cabinets in the museum, underwrite future books as well as make a donation to the Burns Unit. The badges are likely to be future collectibles:

- Strictly limited, minimum production runs that will not be repeated;
- High quality hand laid enamel products, produced by a traditional UK manufacturer (not cheap Chinese imports);
- Classic designs in their own right.

The PARADERS website at www.paraders.co.uk provides detail of the full range of badges and cuff-links available and you can also find a history of City's identity as well as a gallery of original historic badges. Certain items are being sold on ebay (seller identity: Paraders). Also available for sale in bantamspast before kick-off on match days.

Further details: badges@paraders.co.uk / PO Box 307 SHIPLEY BD18 9BT